THE PROPHET HARRIS

THE PROPHET HARRIS

*A study of an African prophet and his mass-movement
in the Ivory Coast and the Gold Coast 1913-1915*

GORDON MACKAY HALIBURTON

University of Botswana, Lesotho and Swaziland

NEW YORK   OXFORD UNIVERSITY PRESS
LONDON   1973   TORONTO

THIS STUDY IS ONE IN A SERIES OF SHORT BIOGRAPHIES OF DISTINGUISHED
BLACK AMERICANS AND BLACK AFRICANS, PREPARED UNDER THE EDITORSHIP OF
PROFESSOR HOLLIS R. LYNCH OF COLUMBIA UNIVERSITY.

This book is dedicated to my wife, without whose encouragement and help it would not have been written.

Contents

Maps

Plates

We are grateful to the following for permission to reproduce photographs as plates: 6 and 7, the author; 3(t.), 4 and 8(b.), the Rev. W. J. Platt; 1, 4(t.) and 5, the M.M.S.; 2, the British Museum; 8(t.), Aux Deux Cousins (Ivory Coast).

Acknowledgements

I WISH TO THANK the following who have helped my research and writing in various ways:

My wife, who has typed and helpfully criticised the manuscript; Professor Roland Oliver, my supervisor; the Rev. Andrew Walls, the Rev. Harold Turner, Dr E. G. Parrinder, Mr Christopher Fyfe, Dr Richard Gray, and Professor George Shepperson, for their encouragement and advice; the Rev. Philip Potter and Miss Brenda Wolfendale of the Methodist Missionary Society; M. Krugère of the Paris Missionary Society; Dr V. Nelle Bellamy of The Church Historical Society, Austin, Texas; the Rev. B. Eerden of the Società delle Missionie Africane, Rome; Dr J. W. Cason of Cuttington College, Liberia; Miss Jane Martin of Boston University; English and Ivoirian clergy of l'Église Protestante Méthodiste in the Ivory Coast, especially Rowland Joiner, D. Parry, F. E. LeNoury, John Turner, Jean Mel, Laurent Lassm, and Samson Nandjui; Mobio Jean, my invaluable guide and interpreter in the Ivory Coast; M. Amon d'Aby and his staff of the National Archives of the Ivory Coast; B. Holas of the Centre des Sciences Humaines, Abidjan; the Rev. F. C. F. Grant of the Methodist Church of Ghana, Accra; Canon C. H. Elliott, Cape Coast; the Rev. John Steadman, Berekum; Mr Ansah, Axim; Mr Polley, Kikam; Mr Hammond, Half Assinie; Mr J. M. Akita and the staff of the National Archives of Ghana, especially Mr Kumi at the Cape Coast branch; finally, many old men listed in the bibliography, who gave the oral evidence which provides a substantial part of this thesis.

Abbreviations

Abid.	National Archives of the Ivory Coast, Abidjan
Dakar	National Archives of Senegal, Dakar
Cape Coast	Office of the Regional Commissioner, Cape Coast, Ghana
Accra	National Archives of Ghana, Accra
P.R.O.	Public Records Office, London
C.O.	Colonial Office, London
F.O.	Foreign Office, London
M.M.S.	Methodist Missionary Society, London
Min. G.C.S.	Minutes of the Gold Coast District Synod of the Methodist Church

Preface

A DECADE AGO, while teaching in Sierra Leone, I first encountered the name of 'the Prophet Harris' and began to look into his fascinating career. Because of the cultural confrontation between Western Christianity and African Tradition, in all senses of both, which I observed around me, I became interested in a man who had found a successful way of interpreting the one to the other. My interest led me to do research on the Harris Movement as a graduate student in the University of London, and the result was my doctoral dissertation, which forms the basis of this book.[1]

Besides making use of archival sources which had not previously been examined, I travelled over some of the area in which Harris had made such an impression, and tapped the stories of the old people who had seen and heard him. Although published accounts described the special impact his presence had on people, their own words conveyed most vividly the strength of the *charisma* he exerted, and still exerts, on the popular imagination.

Before proceeding to the particulars of Harris's career, it would be well to understand what he claimed to be when calling himself a *prophet*. A prophet, in the religious sense, is an inspired messenger of God. From a human point of view, as an anthropologist would explain it, he is a man who feels more keenly than others the problems facing his society, and preaches a saving course of change to his people. If he does not have a high degree of charisma, that is, an unusual or even superhuman degree of power and charm, he may fail to move his society; if on the other hand they do accept him as endowed by God with power, he may, by

---

1. The present volume is a shortened version of *The Prophet Harris* published by the Longman Group in England. That edition deals with the post-Harris period at greater length than does the present one.

his preaching, bring about a change not only in religious practices but in the fabric of society as a whole.

In our western world our leaders in social change have generally been politicians and their charisma, such as it is, shows itself in vote-getting ability; but in the colonial areas of the world there were no possibilities of political action. The tightening grip of colonial administrations could be broken only by outright rebellions doomed ultimately to failure. In certain areas, and in Africa especially, the strong religious element in traditional social structures made it a natural area for the independent expression denied in the political field. It should be obvious then why charismatic spiritual leaders appeared and why the changes they preached were couched in religious rather than political terms.

The Prophet Harris was such a man formed out of a particular nexus of tensions and appealing to peoples caught up in similar, though not identical, tensions. Harris made the focus of his preaching an attack on the traditional religious beliefs of the people, and especially on witchcraft in all its forms.

A brief discussion of the nature of the traditional beliefs may be necessary here, especially since some opinion would deny that witchcraft and wizardry can be counted as religious elements.

While traditional religion varied in its details among the tribes Harris visited, essentially it was one. Although the Supreme Being, the Creator was referred to and honoured, he was not expected to be concerned with the details of men's lives, and in all that region there were probably no temples, priests, or altars serving him. He was the prime mover, but when men wanted help in their daily lives they called on the ancestral spirits or the natural divinities of the rocks, woods, and water. Those individuals who wished to control spiritual forces obtained *fetishes* (or, as Dr Parrinder suggests, charms or amulets[2]): material objects which spiritual forces were induced to occupy, as it were, in a latent state, yet ready at the command or prayer of their owner to become active. Such men have been known as 'fetish-men' (in Francophone regions as *féticheurs*). More exact terms, perhaps, would be 'fetish practitioner', or magician, or sorcerer. Undesirable as the retention of the words 'fetish' and 'fetishism' may be for a correct understanding of African traditional religious beliefs, they necessarily find a place in this historical account since they were terms used by those who described Harris's career, and by Harris himself.

Father Tempels has shown that the African view of the world accepts the idea that there are vital forces, originating with God,[3] which men may

2. E. G. Parrinder, *West African Religion*, pp. 12–13.
3. P. Tempels, *Bantu Philosophy*, p. 30.

usc to strengthen themselves or to weaken their enemies through prayers, magical practices, and medicine. Each man also controls a certain amount of vital force, personal to himself, which he may unleash to harm others by willing it so, or even by simply allowing himself to feel enmity, hatred, envy, or jealousy, for these are indications that he is radiating wicked forces (unconsciously, perhaps) to harm others. To do this is to be, in effect, a witch, as distinct from a sorcerer, who employs charms and medicines to harm others. However, the distinction is not always clear.

Lucy P. Mair, who has analysed the African belief in witchcraft, has shown that it follows logically from the African view that the world follows a moral pattern in which there is no room for chance.[4] In such a world, suffering is meant to fall only on those who deserve it, so when a man whose conduct has been blameless suffers some misfortune, the presumption is that an enemy is at work. In such a case a diviner may be called in to identify the culprit, since there are no outward signs setting him (or her) apart from the rest of the community. This is especially true in the case of a witch who has done this (or her) evil by thought alone; possibly the 'witch' is not even a person but an evil spirit inhabiting and using an innocent person without that person's knowledge.[5] The full terror of witchcraft can be appreciated when it is realised that not only would the individual be ignorant that he is eating the vital force of others at nightly covens or witch gatherings, but that in many societies it is his own relatives whom he is said to kill thus. Among the Akan, if a well-to-do person died it was his blood relatives who were suspected, for 'if a person possessed the power of witchcraft, he used it to "eat" within his own lineage'.[6]

This brief sketch of the religious and supernatural background against which Harris did his work indicates the nature of the forces against which he struggled, that is, the spiritual powers controlled by sorcerers and witches. In a time of social change, such as Harris encountered particularly in the Ivory Coast, new anxieties and tensions were arising which made it seem that evil-doers (both the involuntary 'witches' and the unprincipled fetish practitioners) were more prevalent than ever before, and at the same time there was a general questioning of traditional values and a search for new ones. In the pre-scientific world it is not unusual for such dissatisfaction to erupt into a religious movement which sweeps everyone

4. L. P. Mair, 'Witchcraft as a problem in the study of religion', *Cahiers d'Etudes Africaines*, iv, 1963–64, p. 335. See also E. G. Parrinder, *Witchcraft: European and African* and *African Traditional Religion*.

5. M. J. Field, *Search for Security*, p. 36. Dr Field explains that the Akan word *Obayifo* (witch) means literally 'a person who is the abode of the evil entity, the *Obayi*'.

6. K. A. Busia, *The Challenge of Africa*, p. 23.

along with it, and this, it will be seen, was what happened when the Prophet Harris preached his message in the Ivory Coast.

The Munkukusa or Mukunguna movement in the Congo in 1951–53 was inspired by the belief in the prevalence of witchcraft. The ceremonial obliged the participants to wallow with their mouths in filth and grave-earth, swearing an oath never to repeat their crime of witchcraft. The rite was originated by a husband whose wife had deserted him after their child died. She had accused him of having been a witch and of having eaten the soul of the child; he cleverly insisted that they had done it together and should together take this oath not to do it again. The rite became the fashion as people reasoned that if *everybody* took it there would be no deaths from witchcraft and no more crops damaged by witch-directed animals. When in time it became obvious that death still existed, the cleansing ceremonies became institutionalised with a weekly service combining pagan and Christian ceremonies.

In Ghana, certainly among the more prosperous countries in black Africa, Dr M. J. Field was told by an intelligent and educated third-generation Christian that 'the country had become very unsettled and unsafe, witchcraft was spreading to seaside areas where it was formerly unknown and that precautions must be taken against it'.[7] There a solution has been found in the setting up of new shrines, where the mentally disturbed who believe they are witches are encouraged to confess and be absolved or purified. Dr Field's theory is that the self-confessed witches of Ashanti are the same type of people as those in Britain who give themselves up to the police and confess to being the cause of death and misery to their loved ones and others. In Britain this condition is termed 'depression', and with treatment the patient recovers. In Africa, where the culture accepts the existence of witches, their self-accusations are taken seriously. Dr Field argues that the tensions of increased education, mobility, reliance on money crops, and the strains developing in the traditional matrilineal culture, reveal much more than formerly the mentally abnormal (witches) but also subject the mentally healthy to changes of fortune for which the readiest explanation is witchcraft and evil spirits.

The striking thing about the career of the Prophet Harris was that he offered a solution to the problem of witches and fetishmen much more

---

7. Field, p. 54. B. Malinowski, *The Dynamics of Culture Change*, p. 97, suggested that the belief in witchcraft was 'a symptom of economic distress, of social tension, or political or social oppression', conditions in which a society demanded scapegoats as in the 1930s the Jews were scapegoats in Germany and the Trotskyites in Russia. This suggestion taken alone simplifies too much; in Africa when there is tension and distress witches are suspected, but for reasons which stem from the core of African religious belief.

hopeful and capable of constant evolution, as society changed, than did the Munkukusa Movement or the new healing shrines in Ghana. In the Ivory Coast he swept away the traditional spirits so forcefully and demonstrated the power of God so convincingly that he brought about a social revolution based on a purer moral code and a religious faith more equipped to deal with a changed society. The effect was so complete that for tens of thousands, who had known nothing of any other religion, belief in the traditional world of gods and spirits suddenly ceased; sanctions based on those beliefs crumbled, the old taboos were ignored, and people were free to build a new order. The extent to which they did so varied greatly from area to area, depending on the particular social and historical circumstances of each.

The following chapters indicate how the Prophet Harris emerged as the product of the colonial experience of a Liberian tribe and discuss the characteristics of the peoples he influenced in the Ivory Coast and Western Ghana. Finally, the subsequent histories of these people are outlined. Some tried to use the new found solidarity to retreat into the pre-colonial past, while others took advantage of their opportunity to lessen the tensions of the colonial situation by adapting to it and moving forward, as Harris had certainly intended.

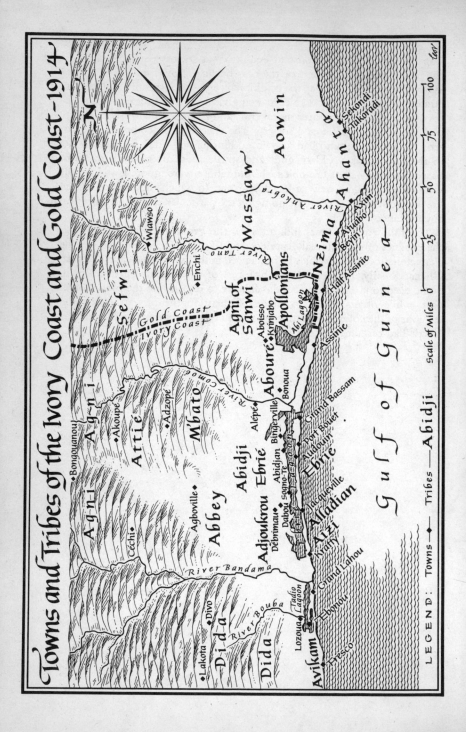

Towns and Tribes of the Ivory Coast and Gold Coast - 1914

N

Aowin

Ahanta

Sekondi
Takoradi

Wassaw

Sefwi

Wiawso

River Ankobra

Axim

Ahuabo

Beyin

Nzima

Half Assinie

Enchi

River Tano

Apollonians

Gold Coast
Ivory Coast

Agni of
Sanwi

Abi Lagoon

Assinie

Aboisso

Krinjabo

Agni

Bongouanou

Akoupé

Aboure

Bonoua

Attié

Adzopé

River Comoé

Alepé

Mbato

Bingerville

Grand Bassam

Abidji

Ebrié

Abidjan

Port Bouet

Alddoun

Ebrié

Céchi

Agboville

Adjoukrou

Débrimau

Dabou Sogno-te

Jacqueville

Grand Lahou

Abbey

Aizi

Alladian

Gulf of Guinea

Divo

River Bandama

River Bouba

Tadio
Lagoon

Kyafry

Ebonou

Lakota

Dida

Dida

Lozoua

Avikam

Tresco

Scale of Miles 0   25   50   75   100

LEGEND: Towns ◆   Tribes — Abidji

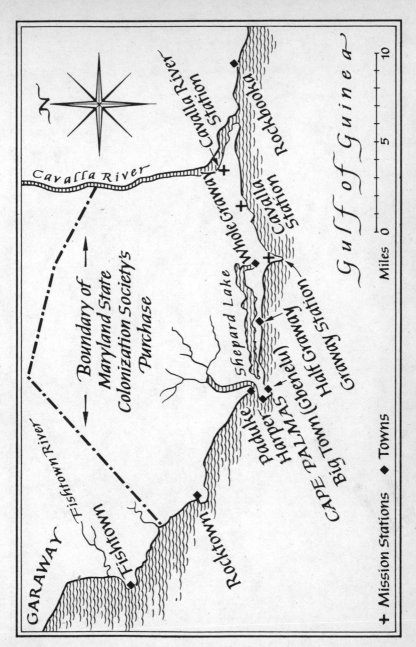

Grebo Country. Maryland in Liberia as shown on map compiled in 1849.

THE PROPHET HARRIS

Introduction

IN 1914 the well-known barrister and nationalist in the British colony of the Gold Coast, J. E. Casely Hayford, met in the streets of the coastal town of Axim an imposing figure straight out of the Old Testament. His long white robe, his white turban and white beard identified him as a prophetic figure; the black bands crossed over his chest and the tall cross of cane which he carried in his hand suggested that he was a Christian. He was followed through the streets of Axim by a crowd of people, some of whom fell into convulsions before him, some of whom trembled with the emotions his presence unleashed, while others simply watched curiously. Freely he bestowed on them his baptism from a little basin of water which he carried and thereby calmed their excited spirits.

This was the Prophet Harris. He flashed across part of the West African landscape like a meteor rushing through the waste places of the sky, seen distinctly in 1914, spotted in 1916 and on several other occasions in succeeding years, until in 1929 came the news that this fiery spirit was quenched forever so far as this world was concerned.

A true son of black Africa, a Grebo tribesman, this prophet made an amazing impression on all who met him face to face. Casely Hayford said; 'He is a dynamic force of a rare order. . . . It seems as if God made the soul of Harris a soul of fire. You cannot be in his presence for long without realising that you are in contact with a great personality.'[1]

Father Peter Harrington, a Roman Catholic missionary in Liberia who met Harris a few years later (1916) at Grand Cess, wrote, 'He was certainly a magnificent type of Negro, the finest I think I have ever laid eyes on.'[2] The French missionary Pierre Benoit, who visited Harris in

1. J. E. Casely Hayford, *William Waddy Harris, the West African Reformer*, pp. 6–7
2. P. Harrington, 'An Interview with the Black Prophet', *The African Missionary*, Mar.–Apr. 1917

1926, wrote, 'This man is really attractive. What a character he has been! Even today, enfeebled as he is, he seems full of energy and power.'[1]

Such was his impression on intelligent and knowledgeable men of the world. How much more were the ordinary people of the West Coast of Africa impressed with him! From 1912, the year in which he began his prophetic career, until his death in 1929, he continually travelled amongst the coastal peoples, bringing them under his spell and persuading them to have nothing to do with spirits, new or old, but to worship the one true God. Countless thousands of people accepted his commands and remained faithful to his memory long after he had gone on. Thousands more, knowing him only by rumour and confused as to his message, yet convinced of his power, attempted to adjust to their new understanding.

It was not until 1922 that the great extent of his influence in the Ivory Coast was brought to wide notice. At that time a young Methodist missionary found that tens of thousands of people had in 1914 and 1915 formed village churches as a result of Harris's preaching, and that they had not, for the most part, returned to the traditional beliefs they had previously held. His reports made the Harris Christians an immediate sensation in devout households in Great Britain and France. Further investigation showed that Harris had enjoyed an equal success in the western district of the then Gold Coast, though it attracted little contemporary publicity. Although no figures are available on his effect on Liberia and Sierra Leone, it is reasonable to assume that he must have aroused a significant response there.

As we shall see in the following pages, Harris was an African evangelist of extraordinary power whose success when measured against that of the white missionaries should excite no surprise. That Harris was poorly educated, that he was fanatical and erratic, that he presented a ridiculous figure to European eyes and that he administered the rite of baptism without the preparation of candidates (catechumens) considered so vital by the missionaries, did not detract from his success but sometimes ensured it. His identification with the people he converted was complete: he was a black man like themselves, familiar with their social structure, familiar with their moral and religious ideas, eating the same food and satisfied with the same material standard of living. There was no serious gap in the flow of ideas between him and them.

If this had been all, he would have been no more than he had ever been, an African preacher familiar with his own people and therefore not under

3. P. Benoit, 'Finding of the Prophet Harris', a typewritten account of interviews with Harris at Cape Palmas, Sept. 1926. Archives of the Methodist Missionary Society (hereafter referred to as 'Benoit's Report').

the necessity of bridging a culture gap. His many Grebo colleagues in Liberia were not inferior to him in that. But Harris claimed to be a prophet with all the special powers which God bestows on those He chooses. These powers enabled him to drive out demons and spirits, the enemies of God. He cured the sick in body and mind by driving out the evil beings preying on them. Those who practised black magic had to confess and repent or he made them mad. He had all the power of the fetishmen and more: with his basin of Holy Water he put God's seal on those who repented and accepted baptism. If after that they fell into the old wickedness, they died or went mad.

He believed God had given him other powers, more dramatic assertions of their relationship, notably the power to call down fire and rain from heaven. These powers gave him an advantage over the missionaries because he showed his power over the spirits and did not ask people to act on blind faith. He completely discredited the old gods as he introduced his God. He kept his converts in the new faith by modifying their practices in intelligent ways, rather than by condemning them outright. A very important element in the lasting success of his work was that he did not have to drive wedges into the social body, as missionaries commonly did, to win over individual souls. Rather he won over the whole community and preserved its social structure intact. This meant that whereas mission converts had to leap over a great gulf separating their old beliefs and activities from the new ones, the Harris converts had only to take a step—a substitution of God for the former pantheon of gods and spirits, and an observance of God's taboos in the place of theirs. The men who had led the community in observing the old faiths led them in the new; it was not those who followed Harris who defied community feeling but those who held to the old ways.

This first step was not, as we shall see, the end. The first step was the beginning of change. The social structure was modified in the course of time as the idea of change took root. Youth rebelled against age and experience in new and unexpected ways. Yet for the most part the new dispensation of Harris survived intact among the majority of the villages for a decade or more; it was he who had broken the power of the spirits and, though subsequent 'prophets' appeared, his image dominated, as it does to this day.

As will be shown later, the peoples of the Ivory Coast responded more completely than any other group to the Prophet Harris. They, at the time of his coming, had been virtually untouched by Christian teachings, but at the same time were being exposed to pressures exerted by French colonialism, to which the old beliefs offered no satisfactory means of adjustment. The evidence suggests that they were searching for new guardian spirits to help them. Their culture, their self-esteem, their whole future as a living people trembled in the balance. The Prophet Harris put them on the new paths they were seeking and helped them over this very rough patch.

William Wade Harris declared that he was a prophet in 1911 or 1912, when he was about forty-seven years old. It seems reasonable to suppose that Harris before that time was in embryo the magnificent figure, hurling thunderbolts and anathemas, that he later became. There is no detailed account of his life, and one can only follow its course by occasional references which have been preserved. Fortunately we know of certain crucial points in his life, the most important being his imprisonment at Cape Palmas for hoisting the Union Jack, and his subsequent spiritual experience—God's command that he go forth as His prophet—while in prison. To begin at the beginning, we must know why he hoisted the Union Jack, and this leads us into the political situation of Liberia in his day. He was not ashamed in later days to admit that he had been a political rebel, and while we cannot detail his political activities, we cannot be wrong to look at the situation broadly and see where he had to fit into it.

To begin with, Harris was a Grebo, and a member of the group of coastal peoples generally called *Kru* who provided so many deckhands and labourers to the ships, especially British ships, trading along the Coast. Harris himself made several voyages, possibly for Elder Dempster, Sir Alfred Jones's Liverpool-based shipping line which linked the whole West Coast of Africa to Great Britain and was a seaborne power in itself. There was, in fact, a community of interest and a close link between the coastal peoples and the British mercantile interests.

Next, Harris was a subject of the black-settler Republic of Liberia, whose relations with its black subjects were more akin to those of other settler régimes, such as those of South Africa and Southern Rhodesia, than had ever been anticipated by its philanthropic sponsors. The coastal peoples tried at intervals to foil their Liberian rulers by getting help from their British friends, but while Elder Dempster obligingly defied the Liberian authorities (or perhaps it was a case of the Krus defying the authorities for the benefit of Elder Dempster) the British government generally backed the Liberian government and recognised its right to control fully its own littoral. Therefore, when Harris the political rebel raised the Union Jack, he was fully in the classical coastal tradition, but so far as bringing about British intervention was concerned, it was in vain.

In political terms then, the situation was that Harris's people were restless under Liberian control and apparently wished to become British, while the Liberians were strong enough to prevent the rebellions from being successful, so long as the Powers supported the government at

Monrovia. However, during the first decades of the twentieth century, Liberia was in a precarious position; if she became an international nuisance she would be partitioned without a regret; and if she could not preserve law and order among her peoples she was likely to be considered as such a nuisance.

Harris the political rebel was also Harris the Episcopal catechist and teacher. Born into the traditional society, he had entered, through a certain amount of education, the Christian and western society planted by the missionaries and Afro-American settlers in the Cape Palmas region. He must have been subject to tensions more complicated than those he found on the Ivory Coast. From what we know of him it seems that these tensions were not resolved until the moment of truth which swept over him in his little prison cell. When the political solution failed, he fervently embraced his new role as a religious reformer. His innermost beliefs then came to the fore: the catechist blossomed into the Prophet. The energy formerly dissipated into several channels was directed into the one cry, 'Worship God, and cease to pray to evil spirits sent from the Devil'.

The chief tensions which produced Harris the Prophet have to be unravelled strand by strand, and the following pages will indicate the characteristics of the traditional society and the defiance with which the pretensions of the Afro-American settlers were greeted. The effect of dynamic work by Christian missionaries was that the Grebos produced a westernised élite, educated and conscious of its own abilities and keenly aware of the inferior qualifications of much of the 'Americo-Liberian' ruling class. In 1904 Arthur Barclay, sympathetic to the Grebo aspirations, became President of Liberia with the aim of securing the continued independence of the Republic as well as doing justice to the rights and desires of the native population. The British Foreign Office was anxious to assist in this, since an independent Liberia was more valuable to British commerce than a Liberia partitioned between Britain, France and Germany.

The plan agreed upon between the Foreign Office and Barclay appeared to be going well until early in 1909 when feeling in Monrovia became extremely anti-British and following a crisis on 11–12 February, British prestige hit rock-bottom and Liberia began to look elsewhere for friends. William Wade Harris was involved in the events of February 1909, and it was during that crucial period that he raised the Union Jack and reached his climax as a political rebel.

In the following pages we shall look more closely at the background, the colonial situation of the Grebos and the events leading up to 11 February 1909.

CHAPTER ONE

The Grebos and the Settlers: Conflict and Cultural Assimilation

WILLIAM WADE[1] HARRIS was born of Grebo parents, uneducated and unacquainted with Christianity, around the year 1865. The Grebos,[2] a branch of the Kru family of peoples, inhabit a large area stretching inland from Cape Palmas. Here a distinctive traditional culture was exposed to western and missionary influence at quite an early period, because of the influx of black settlers from the United States from 1834. With the settlers came missionaries, mainly white, whose interest was in the conversion of the Grebos. Harris, born in a pagan home at Half-Graway (Glogbale), where people prayed to the spirits through a rock in the middle of the town, lived for a time with a Christian minister and received the rudiments of a western education at an early age. He was therefore exposed to a variety of influences which had their place in shaping his subsequent career.

Practically nothing is known of the childhood of Harris, but the first general influences to shape him were the traditional customs and institutions of his people. According to their own traditions, the Grebos moved to their present home from somewhere in the northeast, coming by way of the present Ivory Coast.[3] The other related subgroups (the Krus, Bassas and Deys) had reached the same general area before them, and were settled westward along the coast. The Kru sub-group became particularly important as a source of labour on the European ships plying up and down the West Coast of Africa when 'legitimate' trade began to replace the slave trade early in the nineteenth century. But 'Kruboys' were not necessarily Krus, and when Harris was growing up, Grebo youths commonly spent a few years at sea or working as stevedores

---

1. Pronounced Waddy, this is a common Grebo name.
2. Known also as G'debos, Gedebos, or Glebos.
3. Liberia, *Traditional History and Folklore of the Glebo Tribe*, pp. 2–4

in distant ports, coming home with their earnings to settle down at the more traditional occupations of hunting, farming, salt extracting and fishing.

These youths lived in a carefully stratified society, based on age groupings, in which their roving activities were accounted for as well as the more sedentary pursuits of their mature years. Each age group had its individual leaders, but power in the system as a whole was a prerequisite of seniority in maturity and strength. The senior age group provided two leaders. Among the Grebos the war leader was called the *Wodoba*. He was chosen from the family descended from the original founder of the town. Today he is called Paramount Chief. The spiritual leader or High Priest, the *Bodio*, held supreme authority in time of peace, by virtue of his close association with the ancestral and other spirits. This office too was basically hereditary. These two and other office-holders were chosen from among the qualified candidates through consultations with the spirits.

The Bodio carried a badge of office, a *Pleko*, which was a certain kind of monkey skin. With it under his arm he could demand anything. For example, if his people were fighting he would place the Pleko in their midst and the fighting had to stop. On the other hand, his life was hedged around with restrictions. He could not travel outside the area he ruled, he could not leave the town in time of war, he could not eat away from his house nor after six in the evening, he could not shake hands with a woman, nor set eyes on a corpse, nor take part in any pleasure, even dancing.

The Bodio's wife, the *Jide*, was equally important and if he were absent could exercise his supreme authority. Like him, her actions were restricted. Both of them wore black uniforms, a ring of office on the left foot, and like her husband, the Jide carried her powerful Pleko. The home of this couple was the village temple. Here important deliberations took place, here refugees could find sanctuary, and here a fire burned all night for the spirits, both native and stranger, to warm themselves.

Today the Bodio gets little compensation for the sacrifices he makes in personal freedom, but in former times he received tithes of labour, fines, the spoils of the hunt, and the goods brought home by those returning from work abroad.

The fighting men were the *Sidibo*. They included all married and able-bodied men. They were the solid citizens of the town and carried on its business. Under their leader, the *Gbobi*, they performed the war dance and on occasion went to war.

The *Kinibo*, the young unmarried group, were those who went off to sea or to foreign parts. These were presumably the group described by Mary Kingsley as the Kurbo, and she wrote of them:

Known in West Africa as the under-workers in all hard work, as seamen, servants, steward's helpers, in anything but clerking; they have to go and work and get money and what they call learn sense, until they have enough of these things, and are old enough to go back to their country and settle down as Sedibo. The young Kurbo have at home a roughish time of it, their only friend is their mother, and they have to work at home as well as abroad, for no slaves are kept by the Kru people.[4]

An important institution among the Grebos is the family treasury, to which all family members were expected to contribute. Those who returned with wages were counted on to uphold family pride with large contributions. These treasuries were kept intact from one generation to the next, entrusted to the successive heads of family.

The youngest group of Grebo boys were the *Chiennbo*, who kept the public parts of the village clean and ran messages.

Traditionally the Grebo community took a full part in affairs affecting them, and a whole assembly of the people would meet under the chairmanship of the Bodio to adjudicate criminal and civil matters and to impose fines.

These traditional ways of life and thought were one strand in Harris's experience; a second was interwoven when he was about twelve years old. He ceased to be part of his village community and took the first step which led to a cultural and religious break with strict Grebo tradition. He was taken in as a ward by the Rev. Jesse Lowrie, a fellow tribesman who had entered a wider world. His parents no doubt let him go in the hope that one day he would share the secrets and the strength of the settlers who had come from America, and that, like Mr Lowrie, he would have prestige and a position among them. It was a common enough custom for settler families to take in children to whom they gave a home and a certain amount of instruction in exchange for labour. Lowrie, a popular speaker, served the Methodist Episcopal Mission and presided over the mission school at Sinoe (Greenville), a town to the west of Grebo country.

Although Lowrie was a Grebo, his household, like his profession, had many features not derived from the culture of his people. His way of life and his outlook were moulded by two foreign influences: that of the society created by the settlers from America, and that of the Christian missionaries who came with the settlers but were not really of them.

The Afro-American settlements which ultimately united to form the Republic of Liberia were founded originally as a means of removing from the United States free men of African descent whose presence among

4. M. Kingsley, *West African Studies*, p. 447

those who were not free seemed to constitute a perpetual incitement to a slave revolt. So it was that the American Colonization Society, with Bushrod Washington as its President, was founded in Virginia in 1816. This society, backed by daughter societies in other states, sent out the settlers who founded Monrovia in 1821 and called their colony 'Liberia'. The state of Maryland, being dissatisfied with the slow rate of emigration of its own free coloured population, set up an independent society in 1827 and four years later sent a contingent of settlers to Monrovia. On hearing that moral and administrative standards at Monrovia were very low, the Society decided on a completely independent colony, and their agent at Monrovia, Dr James Hall, came to an agreement with the Grebo chiefs at Cape Palmas whereby land was given for such a settlement.

The new colony was founded with high moral aims. Traffic in alcohol was forbidden, which disappointed the Grebo chiefs, and free schools were promised which native and settler children would attend together. While the schools were welcomed, the ban on alcohol was so unpopular that it led to an attempted refusal by the Grebos to supply foodstuffs to the colony. When the settlers threatened force, however, the embargo was relaxed.

In the years which followed, the lives of the Grebos who lived in or near the new settlements were much modified by cultural influences originating in America or in Europe. For example, the settlers and the Grebos around Cape Palmas lived under a code of laws drawn up in the United States with the help of a Grebo councillor during the earliest period of settlement. Various skills were learned by the Grebos in the vicinity, such as carpentry, stone-masonry and painting; they assisted the settlers to erect their stone and wood houses and copied this type of building for themselves. In the same way they acquired new tastes in food, clothing and household furnishings from the settlers, and a minority began to blend with them from an early period, though the distinction between 'civilised' and 'uncivilised', based on an ethnic distinction and not a cultural one, has survived generations of assimilation.

From a purely material point of view, the settlers, therefore, presented a powerful argument for change. However, the real impetus for a change in moral and spiritual values, reinforcing the prestige of the settler way of life, came from the Christian missionaries who accompanied the settlers, not necessarily to work among them but to carry the message among the native population of Africa. Lowrie was very much a product of their efforts, and since Harris probably had no contact with white missionaries while growing up, his understanding of the Christian message and its effects on everyday life were, in fact, derived from them at second hand. Even so, it was a powerful force, for the missionaries had made a serious impact on the Grebo people, shown clearly by the fact that such Grebo clergymen as Lowrie were active in the Christian ministry within a generation of the missionaries' arrival.

The most active missionaries among the Grebos were those sent by the Protestant Episcopal Church. They evidently had no followers among the settlers, and so were able to concentrate on the native population without having at the same time to satisfy the demands of a settler congregation. In 1836 they began their educational work at Mount Vaughan, three miles from the settler town of Harper at Cape Palmas, and as more missionaries, including ordained priests, arrived in quick succession, the work expanded. Mission stations were established in the main Grebo towns along the Coast and along the Cavalla River. The Rev. John Payne became the first Protestant Episcopal Bishop of the region in 1851. He had been in the country since 1837, and learned its ways by travelling about without supplies, depending instead on native hospitality. He perhaps established the power of his God beyond doubt in 1843 when Commodore Matthew C. Perry sent a force of U.S. Marines to rescue him and his colleagues from Cavalla, then under siege as a result of antagonism between the Grebos and the settlers.

For all young Grebos who wished to benefit from the new culture while retaining ties with the old, Bishop Payne performed an inestimable service by promoting the use of Grebo as a written language into which the liturgy of the Church was translated and used at all services. The pioneer work in publishing Grebo material was actually carried on by John L. Wilson of the American Board. His Grebo dictionary appeared in 1839, followed by some of the Gospels. In the year of strife, 1843, when their settler congregation refused to admit Grebo converts, Wilson and his colleagues were transferred to Gabon. Bishop Payne and his successor, J. G. Auer, carried on the work of publication in Grebo, and thus helped to counteract the worst of the disintegrating forces which missionaries and other representatives of a more powerful culture bring to bear on a traditional and pre-literate society. In fact, the very existence of a substantial literature in the vernacular came to seem such a strength to Grebo tribal solidarity that as much as possible it was sought out and destroyed by the Liberian authorities after a few decades.

In order to preserve their flocks from old influences, the Episcopal missionaries, like the Baslę missionaries in the Gold Coast, created 'mission towns' for their converts around their mission stations. Wade Harris while a boy had little knowledge of life in these. His parents were not Christians and in Lowrie's household he was part of the Methodist circle which, while it was influenced by the vernacular literature, was much more identified with the Americo-Liberian settlers and their culture than with the Grebo Episcopalians.

So it was that Harris, while attending the school which Lowrie supervised at Sinoe, became literate in Grebo as well as to a lesser extent in English. Bishop Auer had edited a history of the Bible, some 400 hymns, and school books in the vernacular. Harris was familiar with many of these works, including the history. Harris was baptised by Lowrie but there is no suggestion in the sources that this involved a spiritual crisis, so it seems likely that he was baptised because Lowrie wished it.

After several years Lowrie came back to Cape Palmas, where he evidently had no need of Harris's services, and the boy returned to his father's household. It must have been a shock to leave school, Christian surroundings, and the experience of a differently structured household and its activities. Harris was unhappy in the parental home and as soon as he had matured sufficiently he became a 'Kruboy' aboard ship. Apparently he made four voyages altogether, two to Lagos and two to Gabon. It was at the latter place that he first saw the interior of a French colonial prison, being confined after he broke the strict silence imposed at night around the *Administrateur*'s quarter by singing a popular song in the street.

It may have been during these voyages that Harris developed the sentiment which, in later years, made hoisting the Union Jack an acceptable symbol of his repudiation of Liberian rule. It would seem that a certain bond of sentiment grew up between the young men who left home to go roving and those who employed them. Mary Kingsley, who encountered them in so many places during her tours along the African coast, made a moving plea for British interest in them when she wrote:

> The Kruboy is indeed a sore question to all old Coasters. They have devoted themselves to us English, and they have suffered, laboured, fought, been massacred, and so on with us for generation after generation. Many a time Krumen have come to me when we have been together in foreign possessions and said, 'Help us, we are Englishmen.'

The life of a Kruboy was for Harris only an interlude. He returned to Cape Palmas and thereafter earned his living on dry land as a bricklayer. At the age of twenty-one he followed his brother into membership of the Methodist Episcopal Church at Cape Palmas, his faith having been aroused or revived by a Reverend Thompson, a Liberian (Lowrie being dead). Soon he became a lay preacher. In 1885 (probably) he married Rose Badock Farr and, perhaps encouraged by her, was confirmed by Bishop Samuel D. Ferguson as a member of the Protestant Episcopal Church three years later. In making the change he was not, as one might suppose, moving from a faith of emotion to one of formalism, for the Episcopalians also looked to generous outpourings of the Holy Spirit. One early missionary described one such experience, beginning on 23 March 1840, 'in which adults, children, missionaries, and all present were affected with weeping, praying, and asking for pardon'.[5]

In throwing in his lot with the Protestant Episcopal community, Harris was joining the section of the Grebo community most opposed, on the whole, to the claims of the settlers. In the years which followed the settlement, various disputes had arisen between the Americo-Liberians and the Grebos. During one armed clash, in 1857, troops in canoes crossing Sheppard Lake opened fire on the Grebo town of Graway with the cannon they carried. The result was that the recoil from the guns capsized the canoes and twenty-six citizens were drowned. This was a crippling loss to the settler community and led to a merger with a stronger power. Maryland-in-Liberia had to ask for the protection of the Republic of Liberia, which received her as a mere county and then negotiated peace terms with the Grebos.

The chief cause of dispute seems to have been the question of land ownership, with the Grebos repudiating Liberian claims because, they argued, they had not brought the advantages to the Grebos which had been promised in their original negotiations. An outburst of fighting along the coast on 1875 tried to establish the 'G'debo Reunited Kingdom', and after destroying the settlements of Bunker Hill and Philadelphia, was suppressed by Liberia with American aid. Around Cape Palmas this was called 'the Protestant Episcopal War', since members of that church played a prominent role, carrying a banner inscribed 'In God We Trust' and leading in the singing of the *Te Deum* as the Liberian militia retired in disorder.

It is clear that the Episcopalians had a greater appeal for those Grebos ready to break with tradition than other denominations. They had no commitments to the settler population, they encouraged the use of Grebo as a written language for secular and liturgical purposes, and while encouraging the Grebos to take a pride in themselves, they linked them with the great world-wide Anglican communion. The educational work they undertook among the Grebos soon bore fruit in a supply of pastors and teachers, the first ordinands being S. W. Kla Seton and M. P. Keda Valentine in 1865. These men and their colleagues adopted European surnames (there being no family names among the Grebos) but kept their Grebo given names, another indication of the fact that they were proud of their traditional heritage.

5. J. W. Cason, 'The Growth of Christianity in the Liberian Environment', unpublished thesis, p. 149

Of course, not all Grebos had become Christians. A majority even along the coast laid stress on the role of the medicine-man and of the devil-man or *deya* who, as the Harvard Expedition of 1926 reported, was supposed to be able to find out anything and detect wrongdoers.[6] William Wade Harris worked among people who held to these beliefs and more than once he was obliged to take them into consideration before he acted.

Once he had become an Episcopalian, Harris sought and obtained a post as teacher and on 6 May 1892 was appointed 'assistant teacher and catechist at Half Graway', and eleven years later he was in charge of the Spring Hall School at Graway.[7] Unfortunately, he fell from grace (the specific sin is not noted in the records) and Bishop Ferguson reported in 1904 that 'Satan has been unusually active here, and two of the teachers have fallen into his snares'. One of the two was Harris, and he was conditionally suspended. He must now have been around forty years of age, but Ferguson included him in his observation that 'the young men thus brought under discipline seem determined to give further trouble, but to carry on the work successfully we must take a decided stand on such matters'.[8]

The nature of the offence cannot have been very serious, as the ban was soon lifted and in 1907–08, as well as being Government Interpreter, Harris was in charge of the boarding school at Half Graway where he was responsible for sixteen pupils. The Rev. B. Kedare Speare, who was rector of the parish and therefore Harris's supervisor, had uphill work in keeping the standards of his fellow Grebo Christians at the required level, and on the occasion of the Bishop's visit to his parish in 1908 the latter had to excommunicate seven persons on account of their immoral lives. 'With polygamy and other evils so rife in the country,' wrote the Bishop, 'the native Christians have a strong current against them and are apt to drift down the stream.'[9] Harris, at that time, was never accused of advocating polygamy, but since it was a problem which obviously gave concern to the church leaders among the Grebos, he must have thought about it a great deal and wondered whether Christianity was right in demanding that Africans abandon this ancient institution.[10]

There were other traditional institutions which Harris, following the lead of the missionaries, did reject and fight against, such as belief in

6. R. P. Strong, ed., *The African Republic of Liberia and the Belgian Congo*, i. p. 50
7. Protestant Episcopal Church, *The Annual Report of the Board of Missions*, 1892, p. 159, hereafter cited as *Annual Report*
8. *Annual Report*, 1904, p. 235
9. *Annual Report*, 1907–08, p. 68
10. From about 1887 to 1897, a 'Russellite Church' (Jehovah's Witness) existed at Cape Palmas under the leadership of the Rev. K. Seton, who left the Episcopal Church declaring that he was going to preach the pure word of God. Seton, a friend of Blyden, is said to have preached polygamy to his tiny congregation. Seton was the first representative elected by the Kru peoples to the Liberian Legislature (1887).

witchcraft and the whole process of discovering, trying, and punishing witches. In July 1906 Harris ran into great personal danger when he opposed a local trial by ordeal. As reported in *The Silver Trumpet*,[11] a 'native man' of Half Graway named Bhne was identified by 'a devil-doctor' (deya) as the one bewitching the lake so that nobody could catch fish there. When asked to lift the spell, he denied that he was responsible. He was then condemned to drink sasswood. His wife ran to the Christian community and begged for help. Harris went with her and argued with the devil-doctor, who was a stranger to the area. Evidently he rescued Bhne from the ordeal, but the furious devil-doctor decided that Harris must be tried. A few days later, on 4 July, Harris was seized and brought to the place of ordeal. His friends sent to the nearest traditional priest (the Bodio) at Graway and to the Episcopal rector, the Rev. B. K. Speare. Neither was able to stop the proceedings, the Bodio and his Pleko (his sign of office and authority) being disregarded, a very unusual occurrence. It was not until the arrival of a whole convocation of Episcopal clergy, called from Harper (where they were meeting) by a special message from Speare, that Harris was rescued. Though the mob was held in check at that time, they later begged Speare to bring Harris 'that they might do according to old customs and spew waters', that is, undergo the test.

Harris's later career shows how much he hated witchcraft and sorcery and this would be consistent with the incident of 1906. However, it does seem that in 1908, when he became deeply involved in a political struggle in the Graway area, he was prepared to accuse his enemies of practising witchcraft while seeking a bit of extra supernatural aid for his own friends.

If the records of his trial are to be trusted, he accepted money from the government to act as a peacemaker among the factions causing trouble in Whole Graway and Half Graway. At that time he held the post of Government Interpreter, along with his mission appointments, and was thus expected by the Liberian officials to work in the government's interest. Because of opposition led by Harris the King or Paramount Chief of Graway, King Bulu, had to flee to Harper, and his cattle were slaughtered by his enemies. He had been accused by Harris and his supporters of being a witch, as well as being too dutiful a servant of the Liberian government. On the other hand, Harris is said to have been a member of a group which claimed a knowledge of ancient Egyptian occultism and drew on its powers.

Despite the efforts of the authorities to restore Bulu to office by calling on the superior authority of a more senior chief, Harris retained the loyalty of the Grawayans. He promised to overrule the government's

11. *The Silver Trumpet: a Quarterly Review of the Missionary Work of the Episcopal Church in Liberia*, Cape Palmas, i, 3, Mar. 1907

authority and appoint Bulu's rival, Holo, as their king. Obviously his prestige was immense. The authorities at Harper summoned Harris to explain his actions, and when he did not come they informed him that he was dismissed from his post as Government Interpreter. This put him into such a rage that he wrote defiant letters to the Bishop and to the Superintendent of Maryland County, in which he styled himself 'Secretary of the Graway People'.[12]

It was at this point at the end of 1908 that his destiny briefly touched that of the Republic of Liberia, for his leadership of anti-Liberian feeling in the Cape Palmas region coincided with a state of rising tension all along the Kru coast and what appeared to many observers to be a crisis point in the continuation of Liberian independence.

12. Liberian Archives, *Records of the Court of Quarterly Sessions and Common Pleas*, Maryland County, Book 87, 1907–09. The records of Harris's trial on 12 May 1909 provide all the information on these events of 1908.

CHAPTER TWO

The Cadell Incident

WHILE CARRYING on their own feuds with the Liberians, Harris and his Grebo followers were well aware of the precarious state of the country's position. They knew that in the preceding decades large areas had been taken from Liberia, including lands across the Cavalla on which their own peoples lived. They must have known that such a man as Edward Blyden regarded the Liberians as decadent and inefficient, while praising the work of European colonisers in Africa, and they themselves believed they would prefer to be ruled by white men from far away rather than by the black men on their doorstep. As it happened, the mood of his people and the reckless behaviour of Harris himself came at a time when Liberia faced a crisis and the reiterated aim of the coastal peoples, to throw off Liberian authority by obtaining the protection of Great Britain, seemed capable of realisation. Basically this was a misunderstanding of Whitehall's interest in Liberia, but it was not only the native peoples of the Coast who believed that British ambitions threatened the survival of the Republic.

By 1906 Liberia's inability to control the Krus (by which term we may speak of the whole group of coastal peoples, of whom the Kru sub-group was most important) was causing international concern. The Krus not only were an important labour factor in European coastal shipping, but were significant importers of European goods. By this time the partition of Africa was reaching its closing phase; Liberia represented an attractive area of real estate which would be a desirable addition to the German, French, or British empires. Unstable and weak because of her wretched financial state, she looked abroad for help; without it she could not improve her finances, and without improved finances she could not control her native peoples and present a united front against aggressors.

Arthur Barclay was President during the crucial years when Liberia's fate seemed to hang in the balance. Of West Indian origins, and with a fine record in the Liberian civil service, he had been inaugurated President in 1904 for a two-year term. He soon found sympathetic friends in the British Foreign Office, which felt that British trade interests were well served by keeping the Republic independent.[1]

In his inaugural address to his people, Barclay had struck the key-notes of his policy, to develop the hinterland and to win the allegiance of 'the native populations'. He condemned in his people their constant suspicion of white men and the selfish legislation which had given a check to the philanthropic movement so valuable in creating and maintaining the independence of Liberia.

At about this time an adventurous entrepreneur, Sir Harry Johnston, arrived on the scene and seemed to have the drive and financial connections which would make him a useful channel for the British rehabilitation of the Republic. He had gained control of two interests which help developmental rights in Liberia, the Liberian Rubber Corporation and the Liberian Development Chartered Company. Before he could get more than a look at Liberia, France annexed a large section of the Liberian hinterland, so the British Foreign Office decided early in 1905 to offer direct aid in financial matters and a general support to the Liberian Government.[2] Meanwhile Johnston was to revise his tentative development plans.

The first fruit of Anglo–Liberian co-operation was the negotiating of a development loan with the banking firm of Erlanger and Co. of £100,000, its charges being secured on the customs revenues of the Republic. A Mr Lamont, an experienced colonial civil servant, was posted to Monrovia as Controller of Customs, and soon found himself in difficulties. Without an armed steamer, he could not prevent ships (in most cases from Liverpool) from stopping wherever they pleased along the Coast, and at his request the Foreign Office put pressure on the Liverpool shipping lines (notably Sir Alfred Jones's Elder Dempster Lines) to call only at the officially designated ports of entry. Lamont felt that although customs receipts rose from £37,000 in 1905 to £55,000 in 1906, the latter sum might be doubled if Elder Dempster would obey the law. Sir Alfred Jones finally agreed to order his captains to call only at the designated ports, but made the condition that Sasstown and Grand Cess (where his firm hired most of its Kruboys) be made ports of entry.

During 1907 the Foreign Office formulated two objectives of its policy for Liberia. First, it was necessary to secure a gunboat to patrol the coast, strengthen the hands of the Customs officers, and so get the money needed

1. See D. M. Foley, 'British Policy in Liberia, 1862–1912', unpub. Ph.D. thesis, University of London, 1965.

2. F. O. 367/65, Lord Lansdowne to Sir M. Durand in Washington, 3 March 1905.

for development. Second, they wished to follow this up with the appointment of an English treasurer who would properly use the money collected by Lamont. Expenditures would include the setting up of a constabulary under English officers and then, with control of the finances and armed strength, 'we should practically have secured the country without incurring either expense or nominal responsibility'.[3] However, an essential element in the plan was the gift of a gunboat to the Liberian Government, and though the Admiralty was ready to release to them H.M.S. *Alert*, laid up at Bermuda, the Treasury was demanding that Liberia pay £7500, a sum considered quite beyond her means. However, Liberia decided she must have the vessel, and arranged to pay for it in instalments.

Despite an apparent rise in anti-European sentiment at Monrovia[4] where people were disturbed by the authoritarian trend under President Barclay, he was re-elected in May for a four-year term,[5] with his amended constitution accepted. In August he arrived in England and during his talks at the Foreign Office was presented with three requests: that he appoint an English official to control Liberia's finances, that he establish an armed force of police under English officers, and that the judicial system be reformed by English appointees.[6] Barclay said he was willing to try to implement the suggested reforms because they would be good for his country. On his way home he called on Governor Probyn at Freetown, hoping that there could be more cooperation. He was rebuffed by the Governor, who was apparently 'ill and unnerved', and Barclay failed to win him as an ally.

Following Barclay's return, the Liberian public accepted the Franco-Liberian Treaty, the agreement with Erlanger & Co., and Sir Harry Johnston's Development Company proposals, and in February 1908 the Legislature sanctioned the creation of a Frontier Force under British officers, along with an addition of three British officers to the Customs Service. They did not, however, put the Treasury under British guidance. Unfortunately, the immediate result of the creation of the Frontier Force under Major Cadell and other British officers was that the more conservative Liberians, suspicious of what the Force might be used for, allowed their fears of colonisation to develop and their leader, Vice-President Dossen, became anti-British, anti-Barclay, and pro-German.

Whatever the Americo-Liberians may have feared, the Kru peoples along the Coast evidently felt that a better day was dawning when British officials appeared in the Customs Service and British officers in the Frontier Force.

3. F.O. 367/65, Memorandum of Clarke, 21 Jan. 1907
4. F.O. 367/65, Wallis to Grey, 22 Jan. 1907
5. F.O. 367/65, Wallis to F.O., 23 May 1907
6. F.O. 367/66, F.O. to C.O., 27 Aug. 1907, and Memorandum enclosed

When the British cruiser *Dwarf* had brought Lamont along the coast in April, 1907, her Commander, Lt.-Com. MacLean, was struck by the pro-British sentiments displayed, and commented on it in his report to the Admiralty.[7] The people at Grand Cess, he said, 'are remarkably intelligent, almost every adult speaking English, they all evinced a strong desire to become British subjects, and freely expressed their antipathy towards the Liberians, saying that they never knew their country was in Liberia before, and that no Liberians had ever visited that country'. On being told that a Liberian Customs House was to be set up, they were annoyed, and said they would pay taxes to the King of England, if asked, but not to the Liberians. 'On visiting the huts of several of the Headmen, portraits of the Royal Family were conspicuous, the natives taking a keen delight in pointing them out to us.' When the *Dwarf* called at Sasstown the people were even more outspoken: if the Liberian flag were hoisted there, they would pull it down; if the Liberians came, they would drive them out, for they were well armed with modern rifles. They said the only people they would obey were the British.

Ironically, it was the British who, through the Customs Service and the gunboat they sold to Liberia, gave the Liberians the strength to bring the Krus under control. In December 1908 the *Alert*, rechristened *Lark*, went into service under a British commander. But the difficulties of making the chief Kru towns ports of entry remained, because of their hostility to Liberia. Moreover, the Krus were unwilling to travel to the open towns to board ship, because of the tribal feuds by which their country was riven. So a season of doldrums set in, with the ships unable to obtain labour and the Krus unable to get the goods on which they had become dependent.

The Liberian Legislature decided to make some examples and punish the Kru towns of Grand Cess, Sasstown, and Garraway by heavy fines. If they did not pay they were 'to be bombarded and demolished, and all communications of egress and ingress to be cut off'. Such were the heady effects of having a gunboat at their disposal at last. The British Consul-General made haste to inform President Barclay that the power Britain had supplied could not be abused in this way, so a gentler means of coercion was sought. It was tested on the inhabitants of Grand Cess. When the returning natives from that area landed at Cape Palmas (then the nearest port of entry) they were imprisoned, fined, and their belongings taken. The British government protested, and in June 1909 this policy was discontinued. Instead, at the suggestion of the British government, Lamont went to Grand Cess in July of that year and persuaded the Krus

7. F.O. 367/65, MacLean to Admiralty, 20 Apr. 1907

to let it be a port of entry for customs purposes. He respected their sensibilities by placing an educated Kru man in charge.

Six months later Lamont followed the same procedure at Sasstown (putting a white officer in charge) and thus the two ports Sir Alfred Jones had asked to be opened back in July 1907 were now legal ports of entry for the Elder Dempster steamers. Sasstown, with a population of 15 000, was the largest Kru settlement in the Republic.

By that time Lamont's position as a representative of Great Britain's determination to remould Liberia into an efficient and stable state had been seriously undermined by the irresponsible activities of the British Consul, Braithwaite Wallis, and the Commander of the Frontier Force, Major R. Mackay Cadell. It was at this point, early in 1909, that the course of William Wade Harris's life was drawn close to the vortex which swallowed up British influence in Liberia and within a year had brought the United States on to the scene as Liberia's chief friend. For Harris it was the end of a period as catechist and Grebo nationalist, and the beginning of a prophetic career which took him wandering far from home and made him known beyond the confines of the Kru Coast.

These events make up an episode which the Liberians called 'the Cadell Incident'. The true facts about it are very difficult to determine. The Liberian view seems to be that Consul Wallis, who, as his reports home show, had a very low opinion of the 'Americo-Liberians', and Major Cadell, who was determined to change the Republic's easygoing ways, conspired with dissatisfied groups inside the country to plot a coup by which Liberia would become a British colony or protectorate. The conspirators supposedly included the followers of E. W. Blyden and representatives of tribal interests. Evidence is lacking which might either establish or demolish the theory that a coup was being plotted. Perhaps the reality of such a plot is irrelevant. The fact that the Liberian government believed that some kind of illegal interference was planned was sufficient to shatter many of the understandings and agreements reached with Britain.

This course of events appears to have begun in 1908 with Liberian fears that the Frontier Force, as it became more efficient, was also becoming a threat to Liberian sovereignty, led as it was by Englishmen and Sierra Leoneans. The Force on its part resented the fact that its pay was always in arrears, and Major Cadell went so far as to warn President Barclay that if their complaint was not satisfied, he would find it difficult to keep them from marching into town 'and giving forcible expression to their opinions'.[8] Consul Wallis showed a similar tactlessness in demanding more haste with the proposed reforms.

8. F.O. 458/10, Consul's Report for 1910, p. 49

Although in his Annual Message for 1908 Barclay had strongly rebutted criticisms of the proposed reforms, condemning the attitude of the governing classes 'toward the outside world, and expressed international opinion', Cadell and Wallis took little account of his intentions and the delicacy of his position as a friend of Great Britain. While cooperating with Britain, Barclay could not risk being accused of disloyalty to Liberia, and his success in walking this tightrope demanded patience and tact from the Britons in the country.

Barclay had also given a hostage to fortune by entrusting Dr Blyden with so much responsibility in negotiations in Europe. Blyden publicly preached and wrote that the Liberian experiment was doomed to fail so long as it was controlled by a mulatto element and not by a pure Negro like himself. According to his beliefs, men of pure race, white or black, were superior to those of mixed blood, for these had a natural tendency towards decadence.[9] From about 1857 his sympathies lay with the native peoples in their disagreements with the settlers (of course Barclay, even as president, expressed a similar sympathy) while Blyden's final lecture in this tenor, 'The Problems before Liberia', delivered in Monrovia on 18 January 1909, gave renewed offence there.

No doubt it was natural that Dr Blyden, when in Monrovia, should visit Consul Wallis and Major Cadell; he was, after all, interested in the reform of the Republic. His influence over Wallis is perhaps illustrated by reference to the latter's reports home in which 'the decadent' and 'lazy' Americo-Liberians figure as perpetual villains, but such visits and such expressions are not proofs of a conspiracy.

The sequence of events in Monrovia during January and February 1909 is not, so far, well documented. In fact, British and American official sources appear to disagree on what happened. Buell, drawing on American sources especially,[10] states that a mutiny of the Frontier Force took place on 1 February 1909, following the arrival of a British gunboat on 31 January. He plainly intimates that this mutiny was intended to overthrow the Liberian Government and lead to the proclamation of a British protectorate.[11]

9. For an excellent exposition of Blyden's thinking, see Hollis R. Lynch, *Edward Wilmot Blyden, Pan-Negro Patriot, 1832–1912*.

10. Mainly *Report of the American Commission*, 'Affairs in Liberia', *Senate Document* no. 457, 61st Congress, 2nd Session (1910). This report may well rest on biased and misleading evidence, considering the emotional atmosphere in Monrovia at the time the Commission made its inquiries.

11. R. L. Buell, *The Native Problem in Africa*, ii, p. 288. Buell does not seem to realise that the arrangements for a Frontier Force were worked out in London when President Barclay was there in 1907, and these included the provision of experienced men, arms, ammunition, and uniforms, which Liberia could not otherwise afford.

British sources indicate that the Liberian Legislature passed acts re-organising the Frontier Force and appointing an 'inexperienced' Liberian (Colonel Lomax)[12] as Commander on 13 January. American sources show that it was necessary that Cadell be superseded because his accounts were in disorder, he had overspent, and he did not obey orders from President Barclay. On 26 January the British Consul asked for a gunboat to protect British property and personnel, and a few days later he asked the Liberian Secretary of State to return all the arms and ammunition not paid for. On 31 January he instructed Major Cadell to have these arms packed and delivered to Elder Dempster, consigned to the War Office, while on the same day he notified the Liberian government that all British officers and men would sever their connections with the Frontier Force on receiving their arrears of pay in full.

The Liberian Secretary of State protested to Consul Wallis on 1 February that his highhanded action regarding arms absolved the Liberian government from any responsibility for them and subsequently the British Treasury had to allow the Foreign Office to write off losses and expenses of £96 15s 10d in this operation.[13] There is no suggestion in these records that these arms were used by the Frontier Force to stage a mutiny and the intensity of the British Consul's plea for help on the next day (when he cabled home 'our lives may be in danger, are we to expect no assistance?'[14]) suggests that he was frightened of rising anti-British agitation.

The Frontier Force did not receive its back pay, and subsequent events were consistent with its desire to obtain it. If there was a plot on the part of Wallis and Cadell, urged on by Blyden, to stage a coup, then it must have been planned to coincide with the arrival of the British gunboat. H.M.S. *Mutine* had been despatched from Ascension[15] as a result of Wallis's cry for help, and arrived in Monrovia on 10 February. On the next day, if we accept the *Report of the American Commission*, Cadell demanded arrears of pay for his men within twenty-four hours, otherwise he could not be responsible for the maintenance of peace or the safety of the President.

On the face of it Cadell was warning that he could not control his men; the Liberian authorities interpreted it as an ultimatum preparatory to a

12. Braithwaite Wallis called him inexperienced. On the other hand, Sir Harry Johnston had expressed a very high opinion of Lomax in a letter to the Foreign Office, 19 Mar. 1907 (F.O. 367/65). Lomax was in command of the portion of the Frontier Force stationed on the Franco-Liberian border.
13. F.O. 367/184
14. F.O. 458/10, Consul Baldwin's Report on 1909, p. 49
15. At the same time, the Governor of Sierra Leone was ordered to send a company of the West African Regiment to Monrovia unless he judged that the situation did not call for it.

coup. Barclay, much alarmed, consulted the American Minister who promised full support. President Barclay then took a firm line and told the British Consul that he wanted all British personnel to withdraw from the camp of the Frontier Force. Wallis by this time knew that his activities were not supported by his superiors in London, and that the Foreign Office was not sympathetic to a pro-British coup. Accordingly he ordered all British subjects in the Frontier Force to resign. They took their belongings from the camp and went on board the *Mutine*,[16] and were subsequently carried away.

These were the events which supposedly should have led to the overthrow of the Liberian government, and Wade Harris, who was in Monrovia in January, was strongly suspected of being one of the tribal leaders who were to raise a general insurrection at the same time as Cadell was seizing power in Monrovia.

As we have seen, Harris came to Monrovia to complain because he had lost his post of Government Interpreter following his antigovernment activities at Graway. On arriving in Monrovia Harris called on the Secretary of the Treasury and on President Barclay, but apparently received no satisfaction and returned home in a state of high excitement. At this time his eldest daughter had a child, his first grandchild,[17] and he is said to have told an official that he was now ready to die. However, when rebuked for not wearing shoes, and thus injuring his dignity as a missionary, Harris is said to have replied, 'When you see me again you will see me with a big cloth on. . . . Look here, I am going back into heathenism. I am going to take off all these clothes.'[2]

A few days later (according to some accounts 11 February, although court records say the 13th), while Monrovia was in a state of excitement on discovering a British warship in the harbour, Harris is said to have publicly desecrated the flag of Liberia[18] and to have planted a pole with the Union Jack flying from it on Paduke Beach, in full view of the town of Harper across the water. With him was a band of followers; their spirits were excited by the sounds of drums and brass instruments, and they shouted insulting and obscene things at the Americo-Liberians who watched them.

Owing to the control exerted by some older Liberians, fighting did not break out as Harris had intended, and later he was quietly arrested and tried for treason by a jury. At the trial some attempts were made to link his action to his visit to President Barclay, but no serious evidence was

16. F.O. 458/10
17. This was presumably Annie, daughter of Grace (Harris) Neal. W. W. Harris had 3 sons and 3 daughters by his wife Rose.
18. Liberian Archives, *Records of the Court of Quarterly Sessions and Common Pleas*

produced to show a connection. The suspicion may have remained, but the man whom rumour said had incited Harris was not even mentioned in court; he was Edward Wilmot Blyden.

Harris was put in prison where he remained for more than a year, perhaps longer, and this heavy punishment for an action which in itself had no serious consequences was because the Liberian authorities were convinced that the Wallis–Cadell–Blyden triumvirate had planned a Grebo rising to coincide with the coup in Monrovia, with Harris as their instrument to rouse the Grebos.[19] This is indicated, not in the records of his trial, but in other statements and writings by leading Liberians.

According to a writer in the Monrovia paper *African League*, Harris, when questioned on the flag-raising by the authorities,

> gives as an excuse that he was directed and advised to do so by one who is called Liberia's greatest and most learned man—a man who spends more time in England than he does in Liberia ... who it is believed is a member of the British diplomatic corps notwithstanding his pretended Liberian citizenship; a man who when he was in Monrovia during the Legislature last January only visited the British Consul, and Maj. Cadell in the Liberian barracks; the man who took an English steamer for the Leeward just before the memorable 11th day of February, and it is said announced in Bassa harbor that Liberia was gone. That is the man that Harris said told him to hoist the British flag on the 11th day of February, the day of the 'hot times in Monrovia'. Was Cadell's movement and Harris' hoisting of the British flag a mere incident? Or was it pre-arranged? People don't ride British steamers free for nothing.[20]

A year later, the Rev. S. D. Ferguson, Jr, of Cape Palmas referred in a pamphlet to the Cadell Incident and continued:

> Simultaneous with this event one Harris, a civilized Grebo of the same Cape Palmas tribe, who had been discharged from his position of Government Interpreter and mission school teacher on account of instigating an uprising between two factions of the Graway tribe, and had gone to Monrovia, was tutored, it is said, by the English con-

19. About this time, Blyden's pension of four hundred dollars, awarded in 1907, was withdrawn. According to Lynch, *Edward Wilmot Blyden*, p. 170, this was done 'on the grounds that he was party to a plot to put Liberia under a British Protectorate'. Fortunately for him, the neighbouring British colonies granted him a pension of about the same amount soon after he lost his Liberian one. It was given for his 'services to literature' at a time when the old man (seventy-seven) was ill and destitute.

20. *African League*, x, 12 (June 1909): only known copy in New York Public Library, where it was seen and the above quotation brought to my attention by Miss Jane Martin. Probably the writer was the editor, a Mr Green. Actually, Sir Alfred Jones allowed Blyden a free first class passage on his ships whenever he required it.

spirators to return home and induce his people to go under the British rule, and that on a certain date Monrovia the capital would fall into the English's hands and the Cape Palmas Grebos were to hoist the English flag as an indication of their fealty to the English Government. He returned home, saw his people, and sure enough on the day agreed upon Mr Harris himself hoisted the said flag on Paduke Beach thinking the plan was being carried out in Monrovia as had been explained to him.[21]

As we shall see, there was a rising among the Grebos—but it came a year later. By that time the United States was taking an interest in upholding the authority of the Liberian Government. President Barclay, in explaining the origin of the rising to the U.S. Minister, naturally absolved his government from blame. It was due to outside influences, he said, dating from the Cadell Incident,

> when the natives all along the Liberian Coast, especially at Cape Palmas, were told that Liberia had become a British colony. Believing this to be true, a native Liberian, who is now imprisoned, hoisted the British flag on Liberian territory. It is claimed that he was influenced to do so by Dr Blyden . . . who received recently a stipend from the British Government in recognition for services rendered.[22]

The attempted coup, real or imaginary, effectually blasted the expressed hopes of the Foreign Office that 'Liberia was to develop on parallel lines to Sierra Leone, and oppose a vigorous British civilisation to the advance of the French'.[23] Pro-German and pro-American feeling increased, while President Barclay's influence perceptibly weakened. In May 1909 a Commission came from the United States to investigate Liberia's difficulties preparatory to making recommendations for American help. Vice-President Dossen, who had German sympathies, continued to ride high, and under his direction the Senate and House set to tear up every existing contract or arrangement involving British interests.[24]

During 1909, therefore, the Kru peoples, who had believed that Britain was taking an interest in them[5] and would see that justice was done to them, had their hopes dashed. The Liberians, in possession now of a gunboat to support the efforts of the improved Customs Service, had much greater coercive power than for some time.

21. S. D. Ferguson, Jr, *Letter from King Yodo Gyude of the Cape Palmas Grebo and Reply*, p. 26
22. Record Group 59, National Archives (Washington), 882.00 no. 367, Ernest Lyon to the Secretary of State, Apr. 1910
23. F.O. 403/390, Memorandum respecting Liberia, Feb. 1908
24. F.O. 458/11, Consul's Report for 1910, p. 1

CHAPTER THREE

The Calling of the Prophet Harris

WHILE HARRIS was in prison his people resorted to arms again. It does not seem to have come about through any provocation offered by Harris or foreign interests, but began up-country through high-handed actions of Colonel Lomax and his men of the Frontier Force. Some soldiers were killed by villagers defending their women[1] and Lomax, startled by the hostility he met, fled to Harper and announced that the Grebos were raising a revolution.

While the resulting events partook of the nature of comedy, they involved tragedy too. Soldiers were despatched from Monrovia, and a German gunboat threatened to bombard Paduke and Hoffman Station. Several prominent Grebos living among the Americo-Liberians were murdered. These included B. K. Speare, the Episcopal priest who had been Harris's supervisor at Half-Graway, who was shot on his own verandah, and 'Tailor Kilbu', who was chased into the sea and drowned.

The Grebo Chiefs sent a Memorial to the British Government, asking that their country be taken over and governed by Britain.[2] They claimed that the Liberian Customs robbed them of their scanty earnings, reducing them to a poverty which their own country could not alleviate, and that the Liberians did not help them to maintain peace but, on the contrary, encouraged their inter-tribal disputes. Identifying themselves in a way to interest British commercial interests as 'a part of the great labour-supply people—the Krus—' they explained that it was the iniquities of the 'demoralised' Frontier Force which led them to take up arms and to stockade their villages.

While the British officers in charge of the Customs Houses tried to keep them open, the amount of small-arms fire from the Grebos forces and the bombardment of the Grebo towns by Liberian cannon, including those on the *Lark*, made the landing of goods dangerous, and by early

March the firms at Liverpool were growing uneasy about the safety of their property in the Cape Palmas Region.

The Grebos had no hope of succeeding in their rebellion without British help, and by mid-March they were desperate enough to threaten the lives of the white traders and to fire on boats bringing goods ashore from the anchored ships. Their efforts were in vain. Great Britain was not prepared to move and it was the U.S.S. *Birmingham*, with Vice-President Dossen and Attorney-General King aboard, which hovered off Cape Palmas as a symbol of international interest in the fate of the Grebo people. Since Commander Fletcher wished to conduct an inquiry before he committed his guns to assist the Liberian cause, and this was indignantly refused by Dossen, nothing was accomplished.

A timely loan from Messrs Woerman enabled the Liberian government to send 250 militiamen to Cape Palmas in mid-May and the Grebos, being short of supplies, soon asked for terms. By August 1910 the Grebo forces were dispersed and the militia, returning to Monrovia in triumph, brought eight Grebo chiefs as prisoners.

While the fighting had continued the Liberian government had not permitted the new British Consul to visit Cape Palmas. When he mentioned his intention to President Barclay, the latter

> begged me not to go. Dr Blyden, when he visited the Liberian coast last year, is reported, rightly or wrongly, to have told the Krus and Grebos that the republic was on its last legs, and that the best thing they could do was to ask Great Britain to annex their country. The Grebos had made no secret of their wish to come under English rule, and the President said that if I went there all sorts of rumours would arise about the intentions of Great Britain, and hinted his position would be made even more difficult than it is at present. [1]

While the Grebos fought and lost this war, Harris remained in prison. He must have followed the course of the fighting with passionate interest, and its outcome—the heat of struggle dying away to a complete defeat and further humiliations for the Grebo people—must have plunged him to the depths of despair and soul-searching. It was in these blackest hours of his life that he experienced the extraordinary physical and mental sensations which for him meant that God had sent His messenger, the Archangel Gabriel, to commission him as a prophet.

Years later Harris described these sensations to the missionary, Pierre Benoit. He did not see Gabriel with his eyes, but he went into a trance and felt him speaking inside him. Gabriel said, 'You are not in prison.

---

1. F.O. 458/11, Baldwin to Grey, 23 Apr. 1910. President Barclay was trebly suspect, being pro-Grebo, pro-British, and pro-Blyden.

God is coming to anoint you. You will be a prophet. Your case resembles that of Shadrach, Meshach and Abednego: You are like Daniel.' Then, as he heard the words 'You are not in prison; you are in Heaven', he felt the Spirit descend on him with a sound like a jet of water. It came on him three times. He believed it was the same Spirit that came down at Pentecost, and later told Benoit that just as men had then been made to talk with tongues, so now he was able to talk to God with tongues. His situation was like that described in the Book of Revelation 20:4 ('Then I saw thrones, and seated on them were those to whom judgment was committed') and, as he believed and said to Benoit in 1926 'I too will have a throne now, it will be a prize'. He described himself as being commissioned like the watchman in Ezekiel 33, and when he was released, he went about preaching, 'Prepare ye, prepare ye, Jesus Christ is at hand. Repent ye. . . . I say to all men, black or white, to repent and believe in Jesus Christ. I am the last prophet.'

From his reading Harris knew the Scriptures well. When Benoit met him in 1926 he wrote:

> He lives in a supernatural world in which the people, the ideas, the affirmations, the cosmogony and the eschatology of the Bible are more real than those which he sees and hears materially. He can adapt wonderfully some situation or some attitude of his adversary to a text and find an analogy in the Scriptures.
>
> The great vision which he had in prison made him the prophet Harris. He felt himself enter directly into this world which he knew by his reading and of which he made henceforth a part.

He believed God called him to the highest mission a man might be given, yet his humility was such that he never ceased to marvel that it was given to 'me, a kruboy'. Benoit wrote:

> But he never doubts it, above all he never derogates it. Neither money, nor threats, nor weariness deprive him of the pride he has in carrying through the world the message of the severe and just God whom he announces. 'Burn your fetishes and idols, or fire from Heaven will be upon you.'

The date of Harris's mystical experiences is unknown, but it seems that he was not released from prison until President Barclay had retired and Daniel E. Howard inaugurated in his stead. This inauguration was in January 1912, and old E. W. Blyden came to Monrovia to witness the triumph of one of his former pupils. Possibly Blyden put in a word for the unfortunate man whose name had been linked with his own in the popular mind. At any rate Harris cannot, by this time, have been thought of as a threat to authority.

When Harris came out of prison he followed the commands of Gabriel and stripped off all European cloth and (it is said) taking a sheet and a pillowcase, he made a hole for his head in the middle of the one, forming a tunic, and tied the other into a turban. His appearance was quite unlike any native costume known in the coastal regions of West Africa, [2] and descriptions of him sought in various directions for reasonable comparisons. A Catholic priest wrote: 'He was advanced in years and of imposing appearance. He had a white beard [and] dressed in a white garment like a cassock or a Hausa cloak.' [3] Casely Hayford wrote of his 'loose calico gown with a black tape thrown over and a rough woven cloth of the same material around his neck', [4] while at the same time another observer who recorded his impressions on the spot told of Harris strolling with a portmanteau slung at his side like John Bunyan,

> with a white sheep's skin rolled in his hand and his cross and Bible in the other. He is robed in white in the form of a Roman Catholic Father with two strips of dark cloths slung across his shoulders in the shape of a stole . . . his cross is made of bamboo about six feet in length and covered alternately in with black and white cloths. [5]

Besides this cross, which, it is said, he never hesitated to smash when it was in danger of being revered as the secret of his power by the ignorant, and so often replaced by a new one, he carried a small Bible, a bowl for water, and a calabash, dried and covered with a beaded net so that it clashed musically when shaken sharply.

Outfitted in this way, Harris announced to all that he had been called to be a prophet, and he left his home to begin wandering and preaching. He asked for nothing from those who listened to him save food and shelter. When his word was not heeded he did not hesitate to threaten to call down fire from Heaven. Those who had known him before believed he had gone mad in prison, and his faithful wife died of grief at seeing him thus. In many places, however, where the people had been quite untouched by the missionaries, he inspired awe and fear and baptised many, telling them to go to church and learn what they must do.

He found his way to Monrovia where the French Vice-Consul there saw him 'carrying a stick surmounted with a cross, gesturing and crying or actually bawling out, without any great success, at the crossroads; the

---

2. Though today in the Ivory Coast and Ghana a similar costume is worn by every 'prophet' who preaches and heals in the Harris tradition or an imitation of it.
3. From the journal kept by the missionary Father Stauffer at Axim, seen at the Mission House there, hereafter cited as 'Father Stauffer's Journal'
4. Casely Hayford, *William Waddy Harris*, p. 15
5. *The Gold Coast Leader*, 4 July 1914

scoffers were more numerous than the converts . . . his stay in the Negro capital was not of long duration'. [6]

A quite different impression was made on Father Harrington, who talked to Harris a few years later at Grand Cess. Although, from reading about Harris, he was disposed to be critical he wrote:

> His features, especially, were most impressive, intense dark fiery eyes, and a beautiful white flowing beard; whether or not his hair was also gray I could not make out, as he wore a turban exactly like a Mohomedan sheik. . . . He spoke in perfect English, a very remarkable acquisition for a Kruman, whose English, pigeon English, is usually unintelligible except to the initiated. [7]

At that time Harris was intimating that he had had no education and that his mastery of English and of the Bible had come by the gift of tongues and of divine inspiration. According to the priest;

> His conversation did not betray any lack of intelligence; his manner and bearing showed no symptoms of nervous excitement or hysteria. He simply seemed possessed by a holy horror of fetishism, and by no means prejudiced or pre-occupied by any political sympathies, nor did he appear to be an emissary of any political designs. Whether by autosuggestion or patriotism, or still deeper religious feelings, he seemed to have thoroughly convinced himself that his tribe—the Kru-tribe, scattered as it is on every sea-board of Western Equirotal Africa—was predestined, like the Jews to play a leading part in some 'new dispensation of Christ', and that himself, their prophet, was one of the pillars in the future reconstructed edifice of a universal Christianity.

In 1913 Harris felt called to travel eastward down the coast and to take two women with him as his assistants. They were dressed in white, as he was, and carried calabashes with which to accompany their chants and songs, most of which were sung in the Grebo tongue. On this journey Harris really earned the title of 'Prophet' to which he laid claim. The whole population of the regions through which he passed accepted him as the authentic voice of God, and as His messenger to revitalise their religion and society which, subjected as they were to new and increasing pressures, were failing them in a time of crisis. Harris, whose life had been exposed to conflicting cultures, saw to the heart of their predicament and by communicating his own blazing faith to them, brought a new factor to bear on its solution.

---

6. Dakar, French Vice-Consul Baret, Monrovia, to Minister of Foreign Affairs, Paris, 19 Feb. 1915
7. The Rev. Father P. Harrington, 'An interview with the "Black Prophet"', *The African Missionary*, Mar.–Apr. 1917

CHAPTER FOUR

The Prophet Harris in the Cercle de Lahou

WHEN HE CROSSED from Grebo country on one side of the Cavalla into Grebo country on the other, Harris passed into the Ivory Coast, where for some twenty years the French had been extending and consolidating their claim to sovereignty. His path lay along the coast and on into the British colony of the Gold Coast; a few months there developed his reputation to a lofty pitch, and he returned to the Ivory Coast to enjoy a veritable triumph.

Colonial pressures in the Ivory Coast had become much heavier around 1908, when Gabriel Angoulvant, the newly appointed Lieutenant-Governor, embarked on a policy of forceful suppression of the inhabitants. In order to bring home the fact that they were now subject to France, rebellious chiefs were deported or imprisoned, fines were levied, and bellicose tribes disarmed. People were removed from their numerous small hamlets and grouped into large villages which were easily controlled; a regular conscription for the *tirailleurs*, or native infantry, began in 1912, and other measures introduced or extended about the same time included the head-tax (*impôt de capitation*) and forced labour (*prestation*).

The Ivoirians were pressured to grow export crops, and by 1913 certain areas were producing significant amounts of cocoa, palm kernels, palm oil, copra, and rubber. These export crops brought them a new prosperity, but also new problems of a psychological and spiritual nature as acute as any arising from direct French coercion.

For spiritual consolation and guidance the Ivoirians relied on a profusion of spirits; many were the traditional gods of rocks and rivers, lagoons and groves, but others were novelties obtained at a price from abroad. The Christian God was known to very few. Although the Catholic missionaries of the *Société des Missions Africaines de Lyon* had been in the country since 1895, they had received little encouragement from the anti-clerical administration and had made few converts. In 1913 they had some 1100 baptised members. The only other Christians in the country were the Africans from nearby British colonies, Sierra Leona and the Gold Coast, or Liberia, who were usually Methodists. They made no effort to proselytise among the Ivoirians.

The most westerly administrative area of the Ivory Coast in which Harris was to make a deep impression was the Cercle de Lahou. With its capital at Grand Lahou, which had the chief military establishment along the sea coast and was also a great trading centre, the Cercle was made up of the subdivisions of Lahou and Fresco on the coast, and Divo and Lakota-Zikis inland.

The natives of the coastal area were the tall, copper-coloured Avikams or Brignans, while inland were the shorter, darker Didas. The economy was, for the most part, on a subsistence level. The men fished to satisfy their own needs and offered hardly any surplus for the Lahou market, and they grew yam and manioc and gathered coconuts for their own consumption. Only the oil palms were harvested with an eye to trade. The government aimed at enlarging the interest in commerce and so coco-palm seedlings were being distributed free along the coast, where villages were being reconstructed more hygienically, with wide cleared spaces around them. The people were encouraged to bring in more fish, were warned against the intemperate use of alcohol,[1] and were made to build roads and bridges where these were required.

In the northern area, opposition to the French was still active in 1913 and late in the year the Administrateur rejoiced in the capture of Dago, an implacably hostile chief known also as a dangerous *féticheur*.

The religious practices of the people, which concentrated to a great degree on witchcraft and its detection, were a worry to the administration, and during 1913 several striking cases of its harmful effects were brought to light in Lozoua.

The Cercle de Lahou was a frontier district. Along the coast the inhabitants were at peace and foreign traders were bringing a breath of the international world of commerce which, along with the administration's efforts, was opening the eyes of the people to the possibilities of money, wealth, and possessions. Besides the native populations, there were many Apollonians from the eastern part of the colony who had come to work with the trading firms as lumbermen in the forest industries. They were vigorous, prolific, and not too scrupulous in business, and settled down permanently as planters and traders.[2] Inland, the tribes of the forest

1. Abid. X-39-5, Report of Chef de Poste, Lahou, Aug. 1913
2. R. Grivot, 'Le Cercle de Lahou (Côte d'Ivoire)', *Bulletin de l'Institut Français d'Afrique Noire*, iv (Jan.–Oct. 1942), p. 55

still defended their individual rights as men independent of government and indifferent to commerce.

FRESCO AND EBONOU

When Harris reached Fresco in 1913 he was observed by a certain Mr Morgan, an Englishman who was an agent for Woodin & Co., and who reported later:

> Folks ... were sunk in debased superstition and fetich-worship, and had been so for years. In three days this prophet-fellow—I heard him preach myself—changed all that. Their fetiches were burnt and what was an ordinary African coast village, steeped in superstition, became nominally a Christian town.[3]

Fresco tradition said that Harris walked through the streets holding a great brass tray to collect the fetishes people brought to him. News of his coming preceded him and he was variously described as a 'messenger of God' and, more mysteriously, as 'a great fetish', so when he arrived at the Avikam town of Ebonou (or Petit Lahou) he was not altogether unexpected.

In Ebonou there were a number of branches of such British firms as Richard & William King and Woodin & Co. (both had local head-quarters at Grand Lahou) and it was some of the clerks ('clarks'[4]) of these firms who had a decisive influence on the movement which developed out of Harris's visit. Without them it is doubtful that his efforts could have resulted in the organisation of permanent congregations. In this area the fact that Harris spoke English was useful for his preaching, because West Coast pidgin English was more commonly spoken than French as a second language. One of the clerks, a native Avikam named Jacques Boga Sako, who interpreted for the Prophet and became a mainstay of the church as it developed there, has left a short written account of Harris's visit which conveys a breath of the atmosphere which swept Ebonou. From this it can be seen that Harris caused an immediate sensation; he appeared to the inhabitants to be a spirit, he was so unlike any humans they knew. His white gown and turban, his black sashes, his white beard and flashing eyes, filled all who saw him with awe, and it could be believed that a new god had arrived, more powerful than any preceding ones.

Harris made his way to the house of the chief, Ekpo-Avi-Addi, to make himself known, and then began to preach the Kingdom of Heaven and the existence and power of God and Christ. He demanded the assis-

3. W. J. Platt, *An African Prophet*, p. 34
4. 'Clarks' is a term used with contempt by Paul Marty, *Etudes sur l'Islam en Côte d'Ivoire*, p. 16. He may not have meant the Lahou group but a less respectable assortment further east.

tance of the Christian traders and clerks when he discovered that they met regularly for private worship. Of these A. E. M. Brown, a clerk at Woodin's (a native of Asafa, Saltpond, Gold Coast) became the chief Harris deputy, assisted by J. W. Reffell, a Sierra Leonean working at King's. These Christians had made no effort to convert the inhabitants, who relied on the god 'Zri-Gnaba' of Batchoué[5] (Tabou) and carried their petitions to his shrine there. Besides this, they had many minor fetishes brought from the Aizis and the Adjoukrous; the spirits they honoured included Assoué-Tano, Aschi-Loboé, Aschis, Schékou, Blikpeu, and the fearsome Mando. There was no missionary and no school, so the arrival of the foreign preacher exuding power and confidence and announcing a revolutionary new order was a sensation. People flocked to hear him and when he said they must destroy their fetishes and confess their sins they obeyed him, even those most intimate with the spirits. No one before had made such a demand. They gave their fetishes to him and he burned them, then arranged the people in rows and baptised them in the name of the Father, Son, and Holy Spirit. Some people had tried to insure against a failure of the Prophet's power by hiding their fetishes in the bush, but a strange fire consumed them there and this increased the awe inspired by Harris.[6] While he was baptising, certain women who had been fetish dancers began to shake, but became quiet when he touched them, making the sign of the cross in baptism. Before he baptised he prayed over the water, which he held in a little white dish, setting it down near the cross.[7]

According to Sako, Harris gave as his first text at Ebonou Ezekiel 37:1-14, exhorting his audience in different ways to love their neighbours as themselves and prophesying that a war would come, followed by the establishment of friendship between Black and White.

When Harris had been a fortnight at Ebonou he received such a pressing call from the Dida town of Lozoua, up the lagoon, that he went there, leaving behind his two female companions. He left the work at Ebonou in the hands of Sako, Brown, and Reffell, with Acting-Chief Amessan N'Drin as nominal director of the movement. These men carried on the

5. He was the Earth-God. There was a special feast for him once a year when people from all around would gather at the town and feast on a couple of cows. There was no effigy of him to be adored, but the lesser spirits were present in concrete symbols and were kept in good humour by being given water to drink, eggs, and other food to eat, and by being bathed at intervals.

6. This story was told several times in the Lahou area. Whatever the basis for it, it is certainly believed that Harris called down fire on the hidden group of magical objects. Harris believed it too, as he told Pierre Benoit.

7. Some sources say that Harris read from the English Prayer Book during his baptism. Amon-d'Aby, *La Côte d'Ivoire dans la Cité Africaine*, p. 151

work of receiving and burning the fetishes and administering baptism. Churches were built which people attended, in some cases from six in the morning to six at night without taking time for meals. Preachers appointed by Sako instructed the congregations in their duties towards God. The clerks, being Methodist, taught them hymns which were translated into Avikam, along with the Lord's Prayer, the Ten Commandments, and so forth. The people worked and ate together in harmony, and formed choirs to sing at their services.

LOZOUA

Lozoua, like Ebonou, is built on an arm of the Tadio Lagoon, but considerably further from the sea coast. Populated by Didas, it is the portal to their country and that of the Yoberi, N'Gbabam, Kazerberi, Gondoukou, and Brondoukou. In 1913 it was a considerable trading centre, and the foreign firms maintained factories which bought palm oil and kernels from, and sold imported products to, the natives. The area around Lozoua was said to have a quarter of the population, and at least half the wealth, of the Cercle de Lahou, and its future was extremely promising. The French were still striving to counteract English influence in the area which the Administrateur characterised as the 'last commercial fief' of that nation's trading houses. The firms had for many years been making long-term advances which were covered by future deliveries of produce and this was a hindrance to progress. The leading personages—the old men, the chiefs, the leaders and family heads—were always receiving new advances before the old were paid off, so that they never had a chance to see money; instead, they consumed their credits in purchases of alcohol and other trade goods of questionable value.

In their greed and jealousy, family heads bullied the young men and prevented them from earning on the plantations. This plutocracy of elders was accused of driving the adolescent youths to other centres to look for employment which would be paid, however meagrely. A further reason for the exodus of young men stemmed from the greed of their rich elders for the women, so that none were left as wives for the youths. Along with this went an anti-French feeling so strong that the young men who found work in French businesses were teased and attacked, and developed a strong sense of shame at being connected with the French. Similarly, the employees of French firms at Lozoua were coldly treated and sometimes waited weeks for someone to sell them provisions. Administrateur-Adjoint Bru investigated Lozoua in 1914 and noted these disagreeable tendencies, as well as the fact that the inhabitants profited by acting as middlemen, and preventing the direct contact of producers from the interior with the firms. He also said that slaves were still obtained from

Dida country and sold to all the lagoon peoples, and that old Affoh, the chief, was a wicked and greedy man.

In 1913, shortly before Harris appeared, Chief Affoh had been fined a thousand francs by the Tribunal of the Cercle as a punishment for the prominent part he took in judging and punishing people accused of causing the death by witchcraft of one of his daughters. As her corpse was being carried around the town so that it might indicate those guilty of her death, it stopped first before two young men and then before an old woman, a cousin of the chief. It was decided that she should undergo a more serious ordeal than the more common redwood test. She, however, ran away from the jeers of her relatives and hid several days in the bush. When she came back she said she had drunk the redwood concoction but being innocent, had survived.[8] The two young men were taken prisoner and questioned until one implicated his father, a brother-in-law of the chief. Public opinion settled on this man as the culprit and he was avoided as being possessed by a very evil spirit. He was put in prison but when the French investigated they released him, accused the chief of having misunderstood his duties as family-head and chief of the town, and found him to blame for all the witchcraft excitement.

The first the town heard of Harris is said to have been in a letter from A. E. M. Brown to his friend Ajusu Nobié, in which he told of the burning of fetishes at Ebonou. When the townspeople heard of it they were anxious to have Harris come and rid them also of the fetish burden. Chief Affoh therefore sent men in a canoe to bring Harris. The Prophet twice refused to come, but when friends at Lozoua wrote to Brown asking him to intervene, Harris was persuaded to go for a short visit. On his arrival at Lozoua he was led to the chief and all the inhabitants of the town were summoned to hear him.[9] When all were settled and he was asked to explain his business, Harris announced: 'God has sent me to burn the fetishes.' He explained that his route led along the coast and that he had come inland only because Brown had asked him to. Now that he had come he was ready to burn their fetishes. The atmosphere was tense as chief and people considered their position. The chief sensed that the people were willing to burn the fetishes if he would make the decision, so he made them share the responsibility by saying he was happy to burn the fetishes if they agreed. No dissenting opinion was expressed, and everyone was apparently happy with such an outcome.

8. The ability to drink a prepared poisonous liquid and survive is a common test of innocence, not only for witchcraft, but of any suspected crime. As we have seen, Harris had nearly been put to this ordeal. The bark from which the drink is made is taken from a tree called, in Liberia, the Sasswood.

9. All this account is based on oral testimony of a large group at Lozoua who gathered to explain it in Aug. 1963.

Nothing more was done that day. Harris was fed and given a place to sleep. Next day every household brought out its fetishes. First were burned the fetishes from the chief's compound, the great fetish Gboualegbe, Brengba (which had been brought by canoe from Cape Palmas), Mando, and others. Then those of the rest were burned, family by family.

Although nobody in the town had opposed Harris, the people in the villages around felt they needed their fetishes too much; they dared not let them be burned. The *féticheurs* decided to bring a sickness on Harris and, as their leader, Odu Oke, said, 'If our fetishes cannot do this they are good for nothing'. However, Harris did not get sick and these fetishes were added to the flames. He still met some opposition; one man hid his instead of bringing them in, but his head began to hurt and within a few days he was obviously demented. This was taken as a warning to waverers and after that, as Harris entered the villages, all the fetishes were heaped up and burned by him, and the villagers were baptised. Harris's message to them, in pidgin, was: 'Fetishes dey in town, in bush, in wattah . . . God send me for come burn . . . let no man go worship de fetish for fetish no good.' The people replied: 'You come here to burn de fetish . . . you done burn all de fetish . . . suppose person be sick, how we gon' to make medicine?' Harris said: 'If you believe God, all be nutting. Everyting be fit do you.'[10] He explained that when they went to gather medicinal leaves they should make a small prayer to God, do the same while they prepared the medicine, and again when they administered it. A man treated in this way would be sure to get better.

At one of the villages, Bassepé, there was a big fetish called Tadjo Soko and Harris went there in a company and destroyed it. That night there was a terrifying storm, with thunder and lightning, rain and wind. Harris came out in the open, called on the Lord's name, prayed, shook his calabashes, and sang his songs. The trembling people, witnessing this, were greatly relieved when the storm came to an end.

The next day was also busy for Harris, for he was led, at his command, to the men's bush to burn the fetish known as Dougoudou Brabré. Following this, he baptised two chiefs and the Fanti traders at Lozoua. He chose a site for the church and called everyone together to see it. He told them that on Sunday they were to come to church and do no work. They asked what sort of singing they should do in their worship and he told them to sing their traditional songs, but putting God's name in them.[11]

10. These are quotations, set down as well as I could catch them, given by the old men of Lozoua, who speak pidgin fluently, though not French.
11. According to Platt *An African Prophet*, pp. 143–7, it was the Methodist missionaries after 1924 who induced the converts to revive the old songs which had been put out of mind for ten years. Perhaps, however, the Didas had kept them alive independently.

They also asked: 'Soon you go . . . who will show us? He replied: 'White man will show you. That is why I give the work to clerks.[12] If a white man comes and does not show the Bible he will be a lying man. Wait for man with Bible.' That night a canoe arrived from the Administrateur at Grand Lahou and Harris was arrested and carried away. His work at Lozoua was cut short after about one month. This was probably at the beginning of October 1913.[13] He was carried to Lahou with arms and legs tied, but was allowed to have a coconut to drink when a stop was made.

In his report of the final three months of 1913, the Administrateur of the Cercle de Lahou wrote:

> I believe I ought to mention the passage in this district of a certain William Wadé Harris, a Liberian subject originally from Cape Palmas. This individual, calling himself 'prophet' and 'messenger of God to burn the fetishes' and to convert the natives to a kind of Protestantism seems to me rather a harmless maniac, and if I relate the fact in this report it is the better to describe once more the extreme credulity of the natives of the region and the superstitious beliefs that they manifest regarding everything in the religious sphere. The village of Lauzoua [*sic*] has carried the greater part of its fetishes to the prophet who has burned them: some children have received baptism from his hands and the construction of a hut to serve as a church was begun under his direction. Summoned to Lahou, Harris revealed to me his beliefs.[14]

It is unfortunate that the Administrateur did not think it worth while to note these beliefs; the details of what Harris preached are hardly to be gleaned from any contemporary written source until he reached Axim more than six months later. The Administrateur's account of his success at Lozoua makes very light of his impact there, but it seems he did not visit the town himself. Certainly Harris had not baptised all the people, but since the fetishes had been destroyed the inhabitants definitely expected to be baptised, and their baptism was carried out later by those 'clarks' Harris had delegated at Ebonou.

GRAND LAHOU

According to tradition at Grand Lahou, Harris was arrested because certain fetish practitioners had heard what he was doing at Ebonou and Lozoua and tried to stop him with their powers before their fetish spirits were driven away too. It is said that the uncle of a man interpreting for

12. Referred to individually or collectively as 'Krak'
13. According to oral evidence of fourteen old men at Lahou, Aug. 1963
14. Abid. X-39-4, Report of Administrateur, Grand Lahou, 4th quarter 1913

Harris at Lozoua came to the Commandant and complained that Harris was coming to deceive the people in order to get their money and so should be driven away. In their fear, the fetish practitioners hastened the doom they were trying to avoid, for the Administrateur had at once sent a canoe and guards to seize Harris and when he was in Lahou itself there was no concealing his power. The Administrateur was disgusted by the uproar.

> His presence . . . aroused, during the few days he stayed there under surveillance, an exaggerated curiosity. Chief Latta, more super-stitious than anyone else, among others brought him a succession of trifling presents, swearing to him that he was ready to be converted. He himself destroyed a part of his fetishes. The extravagances of this chief have been such that the greater part of the elders have timidly asked me to get rid of 'the messenger of God'.[15]

The great fetish for the Didas and Avikams of Grand Lahou, as for all the tribes around, was Ziniaba (the 'Zri-Gnaba' of Ebonou) which was believed to be kept under the ground at Manjué, Cape Palmas, where only its personal priest could descend to contact the dread spirit. People went from a vast area to the shrine, bringing objects which were filled with power by this deity, then brought home and worshipped as his symbol. Ziniaba was so powerful that nothing less than a cow was offered to him at Grand Lahou. The people at Lahou observed Wednesday, 'Adabi', as sacred to the fetish, and on that day could not carry a bunch of palm nuts or a faggot of wood in the village, or go to the bush, take a trip, do any work, pluck bananas, draw water, chop wood, or fire guns. On that day the village was quiet; there could be singing but no noisy commotion. On that day women put aside their European clothes and wore Baoulé-made cotton cloths. Because of the opposition of the administration to the spirits, their symbols were hidden and worship was in secret, but Wednesday still remained a day of rest.

It is not certain whether the two women accompanying Harris had followed him to Lozoua or whether they stayed at Ebonou, but they soon joined him at Grand Lahou. However, the party was in Lahou only a few days and it is doubtful whether Harris undertook any baptising at that time. A certain Lambert Ackah appears to have played a large part in the Prophet's subsequent movements. Ackah had been out of town when Harris arrived and when he returned he was informed that 'Warry Latag-bo', a preacher, was in prison. Being a person of consequence in the Cercle, Ackah went along to the Administrateur and inquired into the preacher's offence. He received permission to visit Harris and having

15. Abid., X-39-4, Report of Administrateur, Grand Lahou, 4th quarter 1913

spoken to him and discovered to his satisfaction that Harris was an honest man whose motives were misunderstood by the Administrateur, Ackah called on the guard to release him. The guard naturally refused to do so without an official order. Ackah went to get it, saying, 'Mon Commandant, this is a man who has come in the name of God. It is not just to leave him in prison with wrongdoers.' The Administrateur agreed that Harris could be assigned a hut beside the prison under surveillance. When Ackah brought food and bedding Harris rejected the food, saying that Ackah had done enough for him.

Ackah and a young man, Latta Nandjué (or Gnadjoué) called again on the commandant and asked him to allow Harris to leave the town. It was agreed that Nandjué could take him away. In Lahou the rumour went around that Harris had been freed from prison by a miracle and as he walked around the streets and preached, crowds came to him. When he saw the clerks from the firms listening to him he called out, 'What are you doing here?' (i.e., 'why are you not instructing these people in Christianity?'). During the two days he was free he made no efforts to gather fetishes to burn or to baptise people. Nandjué arranged to take him by canoe to Kraffy and a throng gathered to see him off. He held his cross up high and said: 'I baptise you in the name of God.' And then, pointing the cross towards the town, said: 'Grand Lahou, I came in the name of God and you have not received me. But one day you will see the truth, for it was in the name of Christ that I came here.'

The activities of Harris during the next weeks are uncertain. The most reasonable supposition is that he stayed at the fishing village of Kraffy on the boundary between the Cercle de Lahou and the Cercle des Lagunes. Presumably many people, particularly from inland across the lagoon, came to him there as his fame spread. Lahou, at any rate, had been convinced of the impotence of the fetishes by their failure to stop or kill Harris, and since Brown and one of his colleagues, Thomas, came to preach and baptise in Lahou after Harris's visit, there was ample opportunity for those who wished to embrace the new faith. Brown was accepted as Harris's deputy in all the region and Chief Gogo Latta, who died soon after, was one of the first to be baptised by them.

Tradition says that the baptism given by the clerks was into 'the Church of England', but this congregation split up when the Fantis began taking collections. An assistant named Kojo was sent by Brown to instruct the separatist group and he did teach them hymns and Christian doctrine and read the Bible to them. On the other hand, he lay with women of the congregation in the evenings when they met to sing hymns, and demanded a great deal of money from the converts. This was so unsatisfactory that when Harris came the second time they asked for a new leader and he gave them Latta Nandjué, who commenced as preacher from January 1915. From that time there were at least two churches of Harris followers.

During the first half of 1914, while the ripples of Harris's work were circling out from Lahou, the official reports ignored it, although they reported such items as the opening of a school in the town on 15 April and the great use being made of the newly-installed oil press. Not until 11 July was Harris again mentioned, and this time he was identified as being connected with the Salvation Army. The new Administrateur regretted that he had been hurried out of the Cercle so quickly, 'for the moral evolution begun among our indigenous population, seemed interesting and we could perhaps have profited from it'. He described the marked effects at Ebonou and Lozoua and said:

> The struggle that we have engaged in against the *féticheurs*, particularly dangerous because of the practices of the ordeal and the veiled opposition they lead against our authority, had not been able to achieve any complete result, despite our tribunals and the severe punishments inflicted. In a few days that native obtained this unhoped for result.[16]

Ebonou and Lozoua had continued to be the centre of the Christianising activities of the Protestant and Catholic clerks, and many Alladians[17] had passed through Lahou and Ebonou under the benevolent gaze of the officials. The official reporting this knew of Harris only by hearsay, but he understood he was remarkably intelligent, although his deputies were not particularly so. At any rate, the change taking place in the lives of the people cast a new light on their mentality, which had seemed 'particularly apathetic and indifferent to the whole moral idea'.[18]

By this time Lozoua, the reputed centre of fetishism and the slave trade, was being investigated by a permanent police officer who had ample proof of Chief Affoh's guilty exactions and abuse of power and anticipated his exile. Beyond Lozoua, the inhabitants saw only the burdens of the French presence, and the 'peaceful penetration' desired by the administration could only be effected as its benefits became apparent in the prosperity brought by commerce. Even in the middle of 1914 the greater part of the Dida population had no contact with the world outside.[19]

The influence of Harris on these people was to grow stronger during the next year, although he did not return to the area again. The ideas he brought, as they percolated inland, were interpreted diversely and unexpectedly, and helped to influence the authorities against the new religion.

16. Abid X-39-4, Quarterly Political Report for Cercle de Grand Lahou, 11 July 1914
17. The Alladians came from further east. See map.
18. Abid. X-39-4, Report for Cercle de Grand Lahou, 11 July 1914   19. *Ibid.*

CHAPTER FIVE

The Cercle des Lagunes

FROM LAHOU, HARRIS went to Kraffy, a tiny fishing village on the margin of the Cercle de Lahou, and actually located in the next cercle, the Cercle des Lagunes. The people who flocked there,[1] or to other centres in the Cercle, to listen to him, included representatives of the peoples who lived on the great sandbar which divides the Ebrié Lagoon from the sea, and of the inland tribes beyond the Lagoon fringes. The population of the Cercle des Lagunes included Aizis (or Addiés), Alladians, Adjoukrous, Ebriés, Abidjis, and, inland, Agnis, Attiés, and Abbeys. Most of these peoples, ethnically close to the Agni-Ashanti family, had offered no resistance to French suzerainty, and in fact, as their numbers were not great, they had little hope of doing so. The chief town of the area and its administrative headquarters was Dabou, on the inner side of the Lagoon, among the Adjoukrous. Here, from the early days of European activity along the coast, the interior tribes met to trade with the coastal people (Ebriés and Alladians) who acted as middlemen and traded directly with the Europeans. From 1843 there were French traders there, but hostility developed (probably because the traders left no room for native middlemen) and the natives became pugnacious. In 1853 the French Admiral Baudin 'chastised' the Ebriés gathered at Eboué and following that, a stone fort was constructed at Dabou by Faidherbe. This fort, abandoned in 1870, was reoccupied in 1892 and became the residence of the Administrateur of the district. The first Catholic missionaries came to Dabou in October 1896.

Harris made his greatest impact on the lagoon peoples who resembled

---

1. It is evident that the numbers who met Harris at Kraffy have been much exaggerated by writers on the Harris movement, for only a deputation went from most villages. In many cases it is not clear on their evidence that they went there rather than to Lahou or Ebonou, or that Harris himself, and not a disciple, baptised and instructed them.

one another in their religious beliefs and social organisation. The Adjou-krou may be taken as an example. To begin with, they (to an even greater degree than the Grebo) were strictly stratified according to age groups, each with its particular role to play in tribal life. Most interesting were the old men, the elders, who were divided into four groups: the Milakŋ, the Lêl, the Makpikŋ, and the Ebebou. The Milakŋ were very old, the 'cinders', consumed, without substance, standing on the frontier between the living and the dead. The oldest among them in the whole of Adjou-krou country was the Pap, who exercised a moral leadership in religious political, and military matters. The next class, the Lêl, 'paper calabash', were the conservers of knowledge and of tribal history. The Makpikŋ, 'tree of the palisade' (i.e. planted to strengthen it) served a moral and intellectual function, while the Ebebou actually were essential to the life of the community. They decided on peace or war, blessed the warriors, offered the sacrifices to the ancestors, and called down the rain. Each age group spanned eight years, so it was the youngest section of these elders, the Ebobou, who were the leaders, especially the religious leaders, of the villages. The three age-groups senior to them were too feeble to wield any real authority.

The oldest man in the village acted as Pap there, supreme chief and priest, even though his age group might be the Ebebou. The prosperity of the village depended on him, as intermediary with the ancestral spirits, and when misfortune struck the villagers gathered in his yard to ask him to forgive them for whatever offence they had committed. When he had done so they handed him a bottle containing water or spirits, which he opened in the middle of the street and poured into a piece of coconut shell, which he emptied drop by drop on the ground, calling by name the most illustrious ancestors of the village and asking them to calm their anger. He finished by pronouncing a curse or blessing. The head of each clan and each family played a similar role in his group.

In considering the possible impact of a new religion on such a society, it must be appreciated that the traditional faith did not encourage an individual to put himself in a personal relationship to God or the gods. Individuals belonged to groups, each of which had a certain role to play, and together they made up a complete 'social body with a corporate relationship to the unseen world. As Edwin Smith wrote in *The Golden Stool*:

The Missionary appeals to individuals—aims at securing personal conviction and conversion. For an African to respond means breaking in some degree from his group—an act which he has never before contemplated the possibility of doing. The stronger the cohesion of clan and tribe, the more difficult is the missionary's task of securing individual conversions.[2]

If Harris was to change these people, he had to convince the elders, the religious leaders, of his authority. If the strongest section of the elders, the Ebebou, accepted the new teaching, there would be little chance of the younger members of the village or family being able to maintain the old faith.

A spirit world enmeshed the Adjoukrous. Each village had its particular god or spirit living at one end of the hamlet, or in the nearby river, or in the pool where the women went for water. To the water god they offered sacrifices so that he would always provide water for them, protect all who drank his water, and make the women of the village fruitful. When these things were not given, and especially when the water dried up, it was obvious that the god was annoyed and was refusing his protection. Every river god had a day of rest once a week, when no one went near the water. What was needed that day was brought home the day before.

The great old trees around the village represented other gods, those who protected the village against attack. Before going to war the young men would offer sacrifices beneath these trees. Sacrifices were also constantly made to spirits at certain rocks and other spots.

Besides these traditional gods, individuals and family heads were in the habit of buying gods from ambulating prophets. These prophets would stay a few weeks with the purchaser to show him how their ritual of worship should be carried on. Such powerful imported gods as Mando, Dibi, and Tanou[3] were possessed by a whole village as guardians against witchcraft. They had their own temples, courts of sacrifice, and services. The *sacrificateur* was priest and prophet and spoke to the gods. On the god's special day the priest judged the witches and evildoers gathered before the temple. If there had been accidents or sudden death he would administer the ordeal of poison to the suspects. One effect of the frequent recourse to this ordeal was a constant thinning-out of the populations.

Known of, but far removed from men, were the great god—the sky god and prime mover ('Nyam' to the Adjoukrous)—and the earth god, but they had no system of worship and were referred to only when taking oaths or giving curses or blessings.[4]

2. E. W. Smith, *The Golden Stool*, p. 256

3. Tanou or Ta Kora was the great river god of both the Gold Coast and the Ivory Coast, and was the chief god, after Nyam, of the Adjoukrous, according to Parrinder, *West African Religion*, pp. 56–7. His priests dressed in white and sprinkled holy water on his followers.

4. L. Lassm, 'Beliefs and Customs of the Adjoukrous', an unpublished collection. This substantiates such authorities as D. Westermann (*Africa and Christianity*, p. 68): 'The highgod is, as a rule, not the object of a religious cult and is of small or almost no significance in practical religion.'

This was the pantheon of spirits and gods Harris found among the Adjoukrous and their neighbours, and since it was not strange to him he was not faced with any sense of unreality of the sort which a white missionary would have felt. Harris accepted that these gods and spirits existed but, like the early Christian missionaries in Europe, he regarded them as demons and devils subject to Satan.

The French were perhaps more active in the Cercle des Lagunes in pressing their 'civilising mission' on the inhabitants than in any other cercle. During 1913, the chiefs from the five districts of the Cercle, Dabou and Abidjan Rural along the coast, and Adzopé, Agboville and Alepé in the interior, were gathered together at Bouaké to see the wonders of the new railway and to glimpse the possibilities it held for the commercial development of the colony.[5] It is possible that, as the authorities hoped, the chiefs were impressed by the practical advantages of this railway which had devoured so much of the labour of their young men in the past years, and which had aroused such resentment among all the people, but it is doubtful that they felt gratitude to the French for it. It seemed to the Administrateur, at any rate, that the enlarged view they received of the country and the variety of its inhabitants gave them a greater respect for the unity of power possessed by the French, along with a new sense of their own fellowship or common interests in being subject to it. These ideas would 'greatly facilitate the evolution of native politics, impeded till now by the individualistic spirit characterising the inhabitant of the forest'.[6]

Striving as they were to make the inhabitants plant bananas, yams, and cocoa, and produce more oil and palm nuts, their efforts greeted generally by indifference, the officials hoped that something would jar the population out of its 'inertia'. Some tribes already seemed to be responding. Some Alladians and Adjoukrous were already known as workers and traders, and some Abbeys and Attiés were showing an interest in trade. By frequent tours of inspection the officials made themselves known and, they hoped, liked by the *indigènes*. By the building of roads and the encouragement of the forest industries and plantation crops, with the intensive utilisation of the available labour, not only were energies harnessed and French authority confirmed, but individuals were to be enriched and the economy of the country raised up. In July 1913 the Administrateur could say: 'From this double point of view . . . the method of the obligation to work which has been applied has given excellent results during these past three months.'[7] During the year forced labour was obtained without incident. The Abbeys were reported to be taking the advice

5. Abid. X-46-24, Report for Cercle des Lagunes, 1st quarter 1913
6. *Ibid.*
7. Abid. X-46-24, Report for Cercle des Lagunes, 2nd quarter 1913

given them and were making progress, but the Ebriés were unmoved, while the M'Batos of the Alepé region, who had been grouped in large well-planned villages, were showing a distaste for discipline and obedience. Some were even reconstructing their isolated hamlets and were avoiding the Chef de Poste when he came to visit them.[8]

Such was the tenor of ways in the Cercle des Lagunes in the year before the Prophet Harris appeared to announce the new order in a way which the people could understand. The French, proud to be representing a secular civilisation, offered labour with its material rewards to a people with no concept of life divorced from religion, no concept of regular labour which had no immediate and tangible results, and which had developed scarcely any wants not satisfied by customary means. Yet that old world of traditional ways was dissolving before their eyes, and the Chef de Poste with his constant visits, his demands for the *prestation*[9] and the *capitation*, and his uprooting of them from the little hamlets where they had always lived,[10] represented the death of the old ways and the beginning of some unknowable future.

The people, quite untouched by Christianity, either looked to their gods and spirits to help them against the French or looked to the French to help them against the spirits. In some cases the French officers were eager to head the battle against superstition and there are several examples from the heart of the Cercle of their efforts.

The Chef de Poste at Dabou reported in April 1912 that he had

had occasion to break up and burn, on demand of certain inhabitants, some fetishes which served to exploit the credulity of the natives. Since this fact has been known, they have, spontaneously and in various villages, brought to the Poste to be destroyed many other fetishes, 'mandos' or 'medicines', which were causing an intense dread among the population.

It is to be wished that the total disposal of all these objects, of a composition as unsavoury as of forms varied and bizarre, may bring in train very soon the ruin of the dangerous species of *féticheurs* which has been up to now the gravest obstacle to our civilising activity in the region.[11]

8. Abid. X-46-24, Report for Cercle des Lagunes, 4th quarter 1913
9. According to L. P. Mair, *Native Policies in Africa*, p. 199, the *prestation* system meant that every adult male gave ten or fifteen days unpaid labour on work of public interest, for example, modes of communication, near his home. In practice, the *prestataires* were often carried far from their homes and made to work longer than the legal number of days.
10. Joseph, p. 153, describes this regroupment and details its advantages for the native population.
11. Abid. X-46-27, Report of Chef de Poste, Dabou, Apr. 1912

In September of the same year, his successor in the same district wrote:

I continued, on the 11th of last month, at Débrimou, with the destruction of the fetishes begun and nearly finished in all the region by M. le Chef de Poste Audrien. This operation did not present any difficulty. Spontaneously, the young men and the adults took hold of machetes and went together to the places where some 'tanos' still stood. These were real nests of mosquitoes, which found a favourable environment for their hatching in the tureens and basins full of stagnant and muddy water, in the midst of all kinds of decomposing matter; I have moreover ascertained that in nearly all the villages I have passed through since the destruction of the fetishes, that destruction has been final, and that only a few attempts at reconstruction have been made in spite of the counsels offered by certain old men of the villages to the adult men.[12]

The same man in October added on the subject:

I have again been confirmed in my certainty that the information I furnished on this subject was exact, and if it would be rash to state that certain customs and rites which are not compatible with our civilising activity will disappear here, between one day and the next, it does seem to me that one can correctly, at least as regards this district, foresee an end very soon to the manifestations of fetishism.[13]

Harris therefore was not coming with completely novel demands when he ordered the burning of fetishes. Where the Catholic missionaries had largely failed, the administration had in some cases succeeded. The material power at the disposal of the officials was much greater than that controlled by the missionaries, and these illustrations strongly suggest that the officials were also presumed to have a greater spiritual power, in the sense of being able to control the evil in the supernatural world.

KRAFFY

By the time Harris arrived at Kraffy, in December 1913, rumours of his powers were circulating across the lagoons, and they convinced people that here was a spiritual force greater than had ever before come to the region. If a power existed which could really authorise the destruction of fetishes and the displacement of the spirits attached to them, then it was not the missionaries or the officials but this man who appeared to be a supernatural being himself and yet was extremely approachable. An

12. Abid. X-46-27, Report of Chef de Poste, Dabou, Sept. 1912
13. Abid. X-46-27, Report of Chef de Poste, Dabou, Oct. 1912

account from an Ebrié village not far from Abidjan describes how everyone heard that a great spirit was coming, one who could be understood by all men and not simply by those who were priests or were possessed. Whole families embarked in their dug-out canoes to find this wonder, usually preceded by exploratory groups.

The villagers soon learned that Harris was not a supernatural being. They asked, 'Are you the great spirit of whom they speak?' 'No,' he replied. 'I am a man coming in the name of God, and I am going to baptise you in the name of the Father, Son, and Holy Ghost—and you will be a people of God.' People were naturally disappointed; they had thought to find a new god. The *sorciers*, those inhabited by evil spirits, witches, all tested his power (and its source) by falling into fits, during which they foamed at the mouth and stuffed earth between their teeth. When Harris saw them in this condition, he lifted up his cane cross and held it toward the sky while he danced all around. This apparently baffled the spirits of evil who departed, and the chastened people stood up and accepted the baptism. Their capitulation removed any doubts the rest might have felt.[14]

Members of the Aizi tribe, a small grouping in the area near Kraffy, offer an interesting explanation of the purpose of the calabashes with which Harris and the women accompanied their singing. These beaded instruments were the same as those used in the old days to call a fetish spirit and sing his praise. They believe that Harris had been a fetish priest and knew the power of this instrument.[15] Since it was essential for the fetish spirits to be destroyed, along with the objects they could inhabit, the calabashes were clashed to summon them before the fetishes were burned, and the spirits, imprisoned, were consumed in the flames.

At Kraffy, Harris shook his calabash as he came forward to baptise, then held it dangling under his Bible in the left hand, while on the Bible rested the little bowl which was to hold the water. While the presumed 'wife and daughter' continued shaking their calabashes, he raised his cross to Heaven and said, 'O God, if Thou hast sent me, give me water, that I may baptise those who ask for it.' Then he lowered the cross and as he tipped it, water ran out of the hollow top and filled his bowl. When he touched with his water anyone who was hiding fetish objects, or who was possessed by evil spirits, this person would become crazed and rush off into the bush or struggle on the sand. Harris would drive the spirit out by putting his sheepskin scarf on the person's head and his Bible on top of that. By the same actions, Harris healed those who were sick, and people paralysed for many years were permanently cured by him.

14. Oral evidence of Abraham Nandjui, an old Methodist 'preacher', at Sanfon-Té, an Ebrié village, Aug. 1963
15. Amon-d'Aby, *La Côte d'Ivoire dans la Cité Africaine*, p. 150, notes this belief, and it is mentioned in an appendix in Bianquis, *Le Prophète Harris*, p. 35

Although Harris gave advice about living a new life, his message during his first passage was very simple: God was good, He was Love. The fetishes must be destroyed, all must be baptised and worship God in the church they were to build. He quoted from the Bible which he held before them (though he did not open it and read from it) and said that white man had sent him and would follow him to teach men to read the Bible. For the governing of their churches, he chose the most suitable representative of the villagers who had come, and sometimes he chose eleven other men to assist them. The twelve were known as the Twelve Apostles of the Church, and their leader, the *Chef d'église*, as the 'Peter', though the latter title may have been bestowed by Harris's Fanti deputies. In many village churches the full organisation begun by the Prophet at Kraffy was never established, and the *chef* or preacher was sole director. Probably the Prophet forgot or was too busy to appoint men for all villages, or to tell the people to choose them. At any rate, the ruling age group usually provided the leadership by his decision or, when that was lacking, relying on their own tradition.

The Aizi of the area had thought of men of other tribes as being objects to capture and sacrifice at necessary intervals. Harris taught them to live in peace with these neighbours, who were also children of God. They followed his teaching readily, not only because he performed miracles, but because they tested and proved the truth of his preaching. He said that as God had blessed everything there was nothing impure, so people could travel by paths believed taboo and eat foods classed as taboo. They began doing these things, suffered no ill effects, and consequently believed in the power of God and the life eternal Harris promised.

At Tefredji the chief fetish practitioner was chosen by Harris to be the preacher, and it was he who began the burning of the fetish objects.

JACQUEVILLE AND AUDOUIN

After some time Harris left Kraffy and went eastward again. He passed quickly through a large part of Alladian country until he arrived at Jacqueville or Half Jack, the largest agglomeration of these 'Jacks', who were a people with a long experience of trade with the English merchants (being their intermediaries with the lagoon peoples who provided the palm oil) and had come to use the English language as their second tongue. When the French took control of the area they were anxious that French should supersede English and wished to have a school established there. The Catholic missionaries were asked to take responsibility for the school and with it the advance of French culture and civilisation on the Alladian Coast. Flattered by the trust reposed in them, they opened their school in May 1898. The chiefs were exhorted to send children there, and some thirty-two pupils came under instruction initially.

From this beginning it was hoped that the younger generation would grow up speaking French. Presumably another aim was to plant Christianity in the region, but if there was any successs in this, it was only among the schoolboys.

As Harris walked along the sandy beach he stopped at village after village and spoke briefly of the need to destroy the fetishes and be baptised, but his reception was generally cool and even antagonistic. He did not stop to baptise but told the inhabitants that when they were ready they should go to Brown at Petit Lahou (Ebonou). When he had gone on his words bore fruit, a development which will be described later.

Harris may have stayed at Jacqueville a few weeks, long enough for his presence to attract people, from across the lagoon. An Ebrié named Megnan from Sanfon-Té (a noted fetish practitioner and on intimate terms with gods and spirits) crossed over when his special fetish spirit told him; 'I am not powerful now because God brings a man who is more powerful, so I cannot live here but must go to another country.' Megnan sought out Harris and was baptised, and though he did not take an office in the church, he was a strong and prayerful Christian for the rest of his days.

Presumably, Harris went to the Catholic church and spoke to the missionaries, who saw him preaching and baptising. As at Kraffy, he filled the bowl with water from his staff, in such quantity that it sometimes spilled on those being baptised. What was left he simply threw away. He asked individuals from far away to carry his news to villages he would not be visiting.

Some months after Harris had gone on to the Gold Coast, at least one of his disciples took up quarters at Jacqueville and offered baptism to pilgrims who came from the coastal and inland parts. 'Sam', as he was known, would appear to the crowd, impressive in suit and tie, in the afternoon, announced by the ringing of a bell. He asked first whether all their fetishes had been burned. When the crowd, an assortment from many different villages and tribes, had answered affirmatively (everyone knew that it was not safe to be baptised without having destroyed the fetish objects), they were sent away to rest until the next day. The pilgrims had brought their own food and made their beds in the clean soft sand which covers all the Alladian Coast.

Next day when the bell rang people settled themselves in rows under and around a shelter built of bamboo and palm fronds. Sam baptised them, holding his Bible in one hand and dipping water with the other from a soup bowl held by an assistant, sprinkling the water on the lowered heads while reciting the formula. It does not appear that he taught anything; once they were baptised they could go home.

The Ebriés live east of the Adjoukrous on the mainland, and of the Alladians on the seashore. Like the Adjoukrous, they are governed by the old men; their 'Nana' corresponds to the Adjoukrou 'Pap'. The *chef de famille* is a most important personage among them; formerly he guarded the family fetish, sacrificed to the ancestral spirits, and remembered and recited the family legends. Like their neighbours, the Ebriés were led by their elders, the priests, and teachers of the old faith, into the new faith brought by Harris.

Harris first encountered members of this tribe in Kraffy, but he visited none of their important villages at this time. With his permission, however, the village of Audouin, not far from Abidjan, became a centre for his baptism, through a new deputy. A Fanti trader there, named Goodman, had heard of the Prophet's work at Kraffy and sent two messengers to invite him to Audouin. Harris questioned the two, Gras and Labiou, and when he discovered that Goodman was a practising Methodist, he sent him a Bible with word to begin baptising the people himself. Goodman had no difficulty in gaining acceptance as one who shared Harris's power. Although the villagers had once before burned their fetishes at the behest of the Catholic Fathers, they had bought new ones when sickness came to the village and they brought them to Goodman to be burned again. As they watched them burn, they lost forever their reverence for the spirits they represented, and the two leading practitioners of the old faith became the preachers in the two sections of the village.

When the news of Goodman's power reached the mainland, many Ebriés travelled to the village and were baptised. There, as in Harris's own presence, the practitioners of evil collapsed in fits which Goodman cured by tapping the person on the head three times with his Bible.

THE CERCLE DE BASSAM

From Jacqueville, Harris proceeded quickly along the beach, spending the nights in fishing camps on the ocean side and completely bypassing most of the villages on the lagoon side. He stopped for one night at Petit Bassam, but talked only to the English-speaking people who offered him hospitality.

At Grand Bassam, the largest port of the colony, with a cosmopolitan and predominantly immigrant population, he intended to make a halt. He was accommodated first by a Mrs Hannah Johnson, a native of Cape Palmas whom he had known in boyhood, and by a Mr Polkey. He had hardly begun preaching when he was forcibly brought to the Administrateur of the Cercle de Bassam and ordered to leave forthwith. He flew into a rage, cursed the officer and the sergeant who had arrested him, and prophesied that they would die for laying hands on God's prophet. He was horrified to see ships being loaded on Sunday, and said that a ship would burn there next day . . . and perhaps it did. It had a cargo of coal which may have been smouldering some time unnoticed.[16]

He left Bassam and continued eastward. A week later Cécaldi, the Administrateur of Grand Bassam, died.[17]

16. Benoit's Report
17. J. Hartz, 'Le Prophète Harris vu par lui-même' *Devant les sectes non-chrétiennes*, p. 120. An extract from Father Hartz's journal, presented by G. van Bulck. The date of the death of the Administrateur is given as 15 Jan. 1914; this has yet to be verified.

CHAPTER SIX

The Gold Coast

IN THE GOLD COAST Harris received the acclaim and attention which, spread by rumour, made his reputation all along the coast. Yet the eventual effect of his work there was not so pronounced as in the Ivory Coast. Probably this was due to the weaker colonial tensions and the stronger position the churches had already made for themselves there.

The Axim District of the Western Province, where his work took place, was the home of two peoples, the Ahantas and the Nzimas or Apollonians. The latter name, derived from Cape Apollonia which was in turn named after the saint upon whose day the Portuguese sighted it, was used by Europeans rather than by the natives themselves. Western Apollonia, with its capital at Beyin, was separated from the Ivory Coast by the River Tano and the Tendo Lagoon. Eastern Apollonia, with its chief at Atuabo, was bounded by the Ancobra River about four miles short of Axim. East of the Ancobra was Ahanta country. Originally Busua had been the paramount stool, but in the course of time Axim Lower Town and Axim Upper Town had become very important chieftaincies.

Both languages spoken in the area are linked to the Anyi-Baoulé cluster, and the dominating element, at least of both peoples came (according to tradition) from inland some centuries ago, the Ahantas from southern Ashanti and the Nzimas from west of Tekyeman. The population of the area was fairly sparse and the towns small. The census of 1911 showed the sizeable centres as Axim (3285 inhabitants), Atuabo (780), Beyin (1524), and Half Assinie (1007).

As Axim was the greatest town of the region, it had a much more mixed population than the others. As at Tarkwa and Sekondi there was a settlement of Kru labourers; apparently they had moved on from French territory to escape the *prestation*. Axim's growth had followed the expansion of the timber trade. The great forests of mahogany along the Tano and the Ancobra were exploited, but exploited blindly. Much immature timber was cut, there was no reforestation, and the Forestry Bill which was drawn up provoked so much misunderstanding and antagonism that it was not passed. Axim, which had called itself the biggest timber-exporting port in the world, rapidly declined.[1] In 1913, when there were three British logging companies, two German, and one American, there was so much activity that the market was depressed, and in 1914 there was much less activity. The value of exports in the District fell from £335,841 in 1913 to £216,642 in 1914 and £107,864 in 1915. Imports showed a similar fall, from £158,530 to £130,384 to £67,165 in 1915.[2] Part of this must, of course, be blamed on the war and the shortage of shipping. Whatever the cause, the figures are such as to indicate that there was a definite dependence on the money coming into the region, and that the collapse of the market in the early part of 1914 would have affected a sizable part of the population. Other than timber, there seems to have been no commodity produced for the world market, because in the next few years the administrative officers were making efforts to introduce the inhabitants to the planting of coconuts and production of rice, and cocoa, and, from 1916, copra.

The only two Christian churches to be found in the Axim District in 1914 were the Wesleyan Methodist and the Roman Catholic. The Wesleyan Methodists had been established longest in the Gold Coast, their first missionary, Joseph R. Dunwell, having arrived at Cape Coast Castle in 1834. Dunwell and many who followed him died before they could make a substantial impact, but under the Rev. Thomas Birch Freeman, an English-born mulatto, the Wesleyan Methodists built up a considerable following among the Fanti population and were a major factor in the widespread development of education, commerce and political awareness among them. Since the Fantis were fairly enterprising and better educated than many other West Coast people, they were to be found wherever there was money to be made in trade, along with the ubiquitous Sierra Leoneans. Many of the Sierra Leoneans were also Methodists, so that the Wesleyan Methodist Church had widely scattered nuclear congregations, though no official cognizance was taken of them.

In 1880 missionaries of the Catholic *Société des Missions Africaines de Lyon* began work at Elmina and spread from there. Two years later the mission station at Axim was opened amid general hostility, and the Catholic population of Nzima grew slowly from that time. However, the

1. Axim Record Book
2. *Ibid.*

majority of people were unaware of any advantages offered by Christianity, and even in 1914 human sacrifice was said by missionaries to exist.[3]

The Axim Circuit of the Gold Coast District of the Wesleyan Methodist Church in 1911 had its headquarters at Axim itself, where a large church was presided over by the Rev. Elias Butler, Superintendant of the Circuit. There were other congregations at Essiama, Atuabo, Beyin, Half Assinie, and in the Ivory Coast at Assinie, Aboisso, and Grand Bassam.[4] During 1913 the work was progressing satisfactorily: at Axim ninety converts were made through camp meetings, at Half Assinie a Mission House was built and the new chapel fitted with an organ, but though Half Assinie and Aboisso had flourishing Sunday schools, the others did not.[5]

The Synod of the Wesleyan Methodists was generally held in February, and that held at Accra from 14–24 February 1914 decided that Axim Circuit should be split in two, with a new circuit centred on Grand Bassam to be called the 'Ivory Coast Mission', while the Gold Coast section alone would constitute Axim Circuit. The Rev. H. G. Martin, an English missionary, was to take charge of the new circuit, assisted by J. G. Koomson, an Assistant African minister who had already, as a ministerial candidate, spent a year at Bassam. The Rev. Ernest Bruce was posted to Axim to replace Butler.[6]

The priest in charge of the Roman Catholic Mission was Father Stauffer, from Alsace, who arrived in July 1912, after many years in another section of the Gold Coast. He and Elias Butler were soon on bad terms. The church at Oirkotoe had been built by one of the villagers, old 'Papa' Essien, and presented to the Wesleyans, who were in return to provide a teacher for the village. When they did not do so 'Papa' Essien became a Catholic and asked the Catholic mission to use the church. In April 1913, Butler broke down the church door. Father Stauffer naturally brought charges against Butler and the case was heard in Sekondi on 16 October, 1913, with E. J. Casely Hayford leading for the defence. Judgment was delivered in favour of the Wesleyans, the Fathers being found guilty of trespass. Their petition of appeal was lost and Father Stauffer, concluding that it had been suppressed by the District Commissioner's clerk, felt that the Wesleyans were all Freemasons and too strong for him.[7] His feelings must be remembered when considering his

3. C. W. Armstrong, *The Winning of West Africa*, p. 38
4. *The Gold Coast Annual; or, The Year Book of the Wesleyan Methodist Church in the Gold Coast District, West Africa, 1912*, hereafter cited as *The Gold Coast Annual*
5. *The Gold Coast Annual, 1913*
6. 'Minutes of United Synod and of European Committee—Gold Coast District, 1914'; from 1917 these Synod minutes were entitled 'Minutes of the Gold Coast District Synod and Local Committee', hereafter cited as 'Min G.C.S.'
7. Father Stauffer's Journal

subsequent account of the visit of the Prophet Harris and his relations with Casely Hayford.

APOLLONIA

The people of Half Assinie, the most westerly centre in Apollonia, had heard in advance that 'Professor'[8] Harris was coming. He arrived with two women and, as at first there was little interest, he and the women made a din and announced that he was doing the work of God and that everyone should be baptised. People assembled, and Harris held up his cross before them and asked all the fetish priests to come and take hold. When they did so the spirits came into them and they began shaking. Harris cried out in a loud voice, driving out the spirits, then he rested the Bible on their heads, and later they were baptised. This persuaded many people to come to him. He began by preaching that all who had 'jujus' and were possessed of evil spirits should throw the jujus into the sea, and some did this. When the owner of a special juju was afraid to do so, Harris came and sprinkled water on it. This drove the spirit out and the juju could be cast into the sea.[9] This went on day after day, although not everyone was convinced. The Catholic Father, Georg Fischer, observed his work but said nothing, while the Methodist Catechist, A. P. Organ, warned people that he came from the Devil. Yet his work brought them larger congregations, for when at dusk and at dawn Harris and his two companions attracted people by going about the town shaking their calabashes and singing their songs, the Prophet's only instruction was 'Go to church'.

After Harris's visit, sacrifices to the local deities ceased for a time and the churches were full of converts. The two most prominent fetish priests were women, Kua Manza and Atua. The latter was rid of her 'spirit' by Harris, but later it returned and she resumed her fetish practice. Then she received a nickname, Betua Bendu, 'It cannot be cast away'.

For Half Assinie, the coming of Harris was a real beginning of constructive change. No longer were menstruating women segregated in special huts; they followed the practice of Christians in sleeping at home and working in the bush as usual. Similarly, newly-bereaved spouses no longer had to stay on the beach for eight days. Many more children were sent to school, and cleanliness became highly esteemed. Similar changes occurred in every Apollonian town he visited.

While Harris continued eastward, he was followed by many people who had discovered after his departure that those of their neighbours who were most familiar with supernatural forces had become truly con-

8. Throughout this district the title 'Professor' rather than 'Prophet' was given to Harris.
9. Oral evidence of one of the two Town Captains and a group of old men at Half Assinie, Dec. 1963

The Prophet Harris as seen at Axim in 1914

Ready for the day's work

Baptising a fetish princess

verted. They felt they must do the same, eventually caught up with the Prophet, and received baptism separately from the local townspeople.[10] Harris went on to Beyin where, although as a Kru he was regarded as an inferior, he was lodged in one of the best houses in town, after he had shown his power. The fetish priests tried to make him sick or mad but found him too strong so they, along with all those possessed by evil spirits, accepted baptism. His chief command at Beyin was that people should join a church and obey its rules.

Leaving the capital of Western Apollonia, Harris came next to Atuabo, capital of the Eastern division. The populace had been hearing of his deeds all the way from the Ivory Coast and the native doctors had been waiting to challenge him. They received word that he had left Beyin and confidently assembled to intercept him. Harris met them in front of the Omanhene's palace. He took the initiative by making the sign of the cross and reciting some 'incantations'. In response there came a super-natural thundering from the sky, and from that moment there was fear of the man. Next morning Erzeah Kabie Angem, a leading medicinal healer who used both natural and supernatural remedies, shouted openly among the populace that Harris was wonderful 'and you should obey him'. Presumably, he had tried his powers against Harris in the night and had failed to harm him. At any rate, he was the first person in Atuabo to bring his magical paraphernalia forward, discard them publicly, and accept the Prophet's baptism. The rest of the people, with a few exceptions, followed his examples; those who did not, burned their fetishes later, in private, and went to the Prophet at Axim. Most of the sorcerers, healers, and possessed, remained good Christians and Erzeah Kabie Angem, in particular, became a Catholic on being relieved of his devil, and remained a devout one to his death.

Harris remained in Atuabo for two weeks. In every group which came to him he baptised first the children, then the adults. When people posses-sed by spirits came to him they would tremble. Harris and the two women would shake their calabashes and Harris would dance with the afflicted person. When the power entered him he stopped shaking the calabash, took his staff, recited some conjuring prayers, then commanded the evil spirit to leave the man. The latter would then become sane and normal and would be baptised. Here again Harris issued no rules but told people to obey the laws of the Church: 'I am just baptising you. Those who live by the rules of the Church will have eternal life; those who do not will have death.' Among those baptised was the Omanhene of Eastern Apollonia, Awulae Erzoah, with his elders, at his palace.

10. Town captains and old men at Half Assinie

Soon after Harris left, on Ascension Day, Thursday, there was an eclipse of the sun; as a result, Thursday was thereafter regarded as a holy day and people ceased to go to the bush on that day.[11]

AXIM

Harris made no lengthy stay until he came to Essiama where he remained for some weeks, making several day trips to Axim and other areas.[12] His first visit was remembered by a boy who witnessed it as being attended by a great commotion in the Upper Town early in the morning. Running to the scene, he saw Harris and his women, preceded by half a dozen sheep and followed by perhaps a thousand people, descending towards the Lower Town. He asked the way to the Omanhane's palace and the crowd conducted him there. Then he had a conversation with the Omanhene, Kwame Benti, and his elders. He told them he came from Tabou (Kruland), sent by God to heal sickness and to teach people how to worship Him. He then asked them to explain to him their customary laws. Then, according to his wish, the Omanhene had the gong-gong beaten around the town to inform people that they were to come next morning to be baptised.

Apparently Harris had already made a secret first visit at the request of the chiefs of Upper and Lower Town, who had sent their linguists, bearing their staffs, to bring him from where he was baptising in Apollonia to the bedside of the dying wife of the chief of Upper Town. Harris had laid his white-draped cross beside her and said, 'Take the stick, rise up, and walk'.[13] The woman had done so, and thereafter led a normal life.

Harris evidently found wide variations in the positions taken by the Christian pastors whom he met. When he first arrived at Axim, the Methodist incumbent was Butler, who warned his members that all who had anything to do with 'that false prophet' would do so at risk of being turned out of the church.[14] On the other hand, Butler's successor, Ernest Bruce, who arrived some weeks later, was very friendly. The Catholic missionary, Father Stauffer, was definitely hostile, despite the formal visit Harris made to him in the second week of June. Harris told the Father that he was one of nine prophets sent to convert the world, and that he had been ordered by the Angel Gabriel to destroy the fetishes and bring

11. Oral evidence of Elder Buah Nrezah, Atuabo, Apr. 1964
12. *The Gold Coast Leader*, 20–27 June 1914, and oral evidence of Sub-Chief Tumunli Kwesi of Lower Town Axim, Apr. 1964
13. Oral evidence of J. P. Ephson, Elmina, Aug. 1963, who claimed to have had the story from the woman's son-in-law.
14. E. Bruce, 'I grew up with history', *African Challenge*, vii, 4 Apr. 1957, p. 6

all people to serve God. He had no special church but sent his converts to the one they preferred. The Father understood him to say that he did not baptise,[15] but this, being absolutely untrue, must have been a misunderstanding. Father Stauffer had heard of his destruction of fetishes and of the miraculous cures. Harris was even supposed to have raised the dead. His attitude towards the Catholic Church was somewhat in doubt, especially as there was a rumour that after a dispute with Father Fischer at Half Assinie he had cursed him and made him blind. However, in Axim he spoke well of the Fathers, telling people they ought to do much more for their priests. When Father Fischer came to Axim at the end of June, he was perfectly all right, so that rumour was disproved.

At the beginning of his stay in Axim Harris's relations with the priest were friendly enough. The only fetish objects he did not burn were two wooden statuettes, one of which he gave to Father Stauffer and the other to the Methodist minister. At service on the first Sunday after his arrival in the town, nearly a thousand people tried to crowd into the small Catholic chapel. Nonetheless, Father Stauffer would allow no liberties to be taken with himself and his office. One Sunday morning, soon after his arrival, Harris came to the Catholic Church and stood with his cross while the service proceeded. Perhaps he expected to be invited to take part or to speak. When he was not, and the priest began to preach, he left the building and stood outside under a mango tree. Here he heard the church bell of the Wesleyans, so he went to collect his four women and took them to the Methodist Church. Perhaps he was allowed to preach there; Father Stauffer thought so.

Harris began his day at about 5 a.m., when he would appear on the streets driving a flock of sheep. People from outlying villages would be coming to the market place where he was going to preach, and there he told them that the world was going to be destroyed by fire, together with the people who would not listen to him and those who would not go to church. His wives (or, as the Methodists preferred to think, the 'friends, who served him as musicians or as a choir') shook their calabashes and sang, '*Nyame se bra O bra*' (God says O come).

The evildoers, the fetish priests, the witches and medicinemen in the throng were overcome by fear of the power of the Prophet. When he called on those present to come forward for confession and baptism, these evil ones came shaking and trembling. All suppliants were to hold on to the cross ; sometimes as many as six were clutching it at once and he would let others hold his sheepskin or Bible. Usually he began by holding his Bible on the suppliant's head and recited something in a

15. Father Stauffer's Journal

loud voice. Then he dipped his hand in the holy water he carried and made a sign of the cross on the man's face, saying, 'If you have an evil mind or a devil in you, you know what will happen!' If the person had nothing on his conscience he could go away freely, but if he was attached to magic and witchcraft he became violently possessed. Harris was striking in his patience when some of these people pulled his beard, slapped him, spat on him, and even smashed the cross. When that happened he simply sent for fresh cane and made a new cross. Commonly, when the Bible touched a man's head, he would break into a confession of the names of those he had killed by witchcraft, and of his other sins. Then Harris would put the Bible on the head again and ask, 'Is that all?' When the answer was 'Yes', he was healed, and Harris told him, 'You must go take all your medicines and throw them away. If you go back to these medicines *you* will die!' The fetishes were thrown into the sea or piled on the beach by the Omanhene's palace, where the Prophet poured kerosene on them and burned them.

Once Harris's mission was understood, ordinary men and women thronged from all around, even from Aowin and Wassaw in the interior, bringing their religious objects and medicines in bundles to leave with the Prophet. As many as a thousand new suppliants came every day, and Harris had time neither to eat nor sleep. He would rest for a time in the nearest house, then go to work again.

Casely Hayford wrote a vivid description of a possessed woman being baptised which has been quoted in the publications of others, and deservedly so.

There has been noticed in the crowd a woman who has attempted several times to touch the cross and held back, as if she would rather not. See! she now gets nearer. At last she has touched it, barely touched it. What is this that is happening, Great God! Is it possible? The woman is torn as if by a violent force. Her body is convulsed. She tears at her breasts. Her eyes literally dart from their sockets. They roll completely up and then completely down. Her hair stands on end. At last she falls prone and rolls about in great agony. Harris calmly goes on baptising as if nothing is happening. After a while he goes near and utters a strange prayer. Gradually she grows somewhat calmer. She is now on her feet. This strange man again approaches the agonised soul, opens the tattered Bible and holds it before her face, the while uttering a prayer. She seems to be growing calmer now. But again she is seized by—I know not what. She roars like a beast. Her attitude is distinctly defiant. She is, indeed, menacing. Harris breaks into a low laugh, turns away, and continues to baptise as before. He now approaches her for the second time, and once more holds the Bible to her face. She gradually calms down and then comes to herself. She is now as helpless as a babe. She takes her seat with others of like nature and awaits baptism.[16]

Harris spent quite a bit of time preaching to the crowds, and now and again would stop and say, 'I am receiving messages from God' or 'telegrams from Heaven' and would look straight at the sun amidst a silence.

The Prophet spared no pains in reaching every element of society. An example was his visit to the Asafo No. 2 Company.[17] This company had just lost their captain, Alicoe, and were praying and mourning his death. Harris was at the palace baptising, but when he heard of this he rushed to the scene, still holding his cross, and joined in their melancholy dance. Then he told the people, 'See, I am a professor, sent by Almighty God. I have come and danced with you. You, after the burial, must come and dance my dance too.' Next day, accordingly, all members of No. 2 Company came and were baptised.

A newspaper correspondent who wrote from Axim during Harris's stay there was sure that he deserved every support from the churches. His work was miraculous; he had destroyed most of the 'demi-Gods' of Apollonia. 'Those who would not hearken to him but keep their fetishes from being burnt run mad on the spot, some dying under his prayers.'[18] The correspondent went on to tell of his prayers for thunder being answered, and of his success at the nearby village of Akinin where 'not less than seven-eighths of the inhabitants' were converted after throwing their fetishes into the sea or into dustbins. Whereas the Catholic Church was full to overflowing with new converts, the Wesleyans had none. The reason given by the correspondent was that the Methodists demanded too much in the way of contributions, and the converts could not afford it. Possibly also Butler had not appreciated hearing from Harris, 'So you don't take advice of a Prophet. God will show you lesson! You are my servant. You should come and hold the bowl with which I baptise.'[19]

Butler's successor, Ernest Bruce, was soon on better terms with the Prophet. He told his congregation, 'whoever believes in Jesus Christ as the eternal Son of God and as the only Saviour of the world is my brother and fellow Christian.'[20] On a visit to an out-station, Bruce met Harris for the first time.

16. Casely Hayford, p. 11
17. An Asafo Company is a traditional grouping of young men in a Ghanaian town, a kind of fraternity. In time of war it would form a fighting unit, but normally carried on a friendly rivalry with other companies in the town. Through the companies the young men could influence the Chief and elders.
18. *The Gold Coast Leader*, 4 July 1914
19. J. P. Ephson
20. Bruce, p. 6

When he came to greet me, I demanded to see his Bible. I saw that the book he placed in my hands was the Authorised Version of the Bible, so I warmly welcomed him. . . . Later we again met at Axim. Prophet Harris arrived one day and asked to inspect our chapel. I asked one of our people to guide him. Some of our other members were angry with me for this.

When Harris found the church too small for his use, Bruce offered him the school, which was bigger.

Many fetish priests hid in villages near Axim, and it was said that one who had fled ahead of the Prophet as he came through Apollonia bolted early in the morning to evade him again. An even greater miracle was reported by the news correspondent:

A man had been converted at Ayinose, the seat of demons, by Harris and within two days [of] conversion after surrendering his fetishes, he is now in possession of Harris Bible and a cross and this fetish priest who has no knowledge of English language can now speak English language very well, abandoning the use of his mother tongue, everyone appreciates the work of Wonderful Harris.[21]

The correspondent mentioned also that the chief fetish priest in Axim, after examining Harris, gave up his fetishes and advised all his subordinates to do the same, rather than go mad.

Harris evidently journeyed out some miles from the town during the weeks he made his headquarters in Axim, for he made return visits to Kikam, Essiama, Assenbah, and Ancobra, where he had to force his way through the multitudes who flocked to see him.

Proof that Harris had miraculous powers was manifested, in the first place, when the sorcerers and others who opposed him were unable to harm him. In Axim, at any rate, and at Kikam, a centre of witchcraft, when those who intended evil went to his room at night they found him floating near the ceiling.[22] They fled in terror. Another instance of his powers was that one afternoon he successfully asked God to send rain; he prayed or recited aloud, the sky became dark, and for thirty minutes it rained.[23] When a convert retained his fetish, a thunderbolt struck the room and destroyed it, while another convert, who turned back to his idols, died. Harris refused him a Christian burial, saying, 'God is the Judge'.[24]

In Axim, as everywhere, Harris preached strongly against working on

21. *The Gold Coast Leader*, 4 July 1914
22. J. P. Ephson. According to J. Barnes Christian, he slept suspended between earth and Heaven, where no witchcraft or anything else could harm him.
23. G. A. Ackah
24. Bruce, p. 10

Sunday. This was bound to involve him in trouble with the civil authorities wherever he went along the Coast, for when ships hove to outside the breakers, all labourers were needed to unload and load her, whatever the day might be. The principal labourers were, of course, Krus, and Harris talked to them a great deal. There are varied accounts of his success with them. It is said that he met with them at the home of their chief, Moses, and that they brought him food in the mornings. As a result of his preachings, they are said to have given up working on Sundays for some years. His chief threat was that God would burn the ships loaded on Sunday, and this was said with particular reference to the S.S. *Patna* which came in while he was there, but it is not clear whether or not the ship did catch fire. Casely Hayford wrote: 'With outstretched hand toward the sea he points to the boats working on the Lord's Day, and hints at strange things that are about to happen. A ship in the neighbourhood take fire the same day . . . it is a curious coincidence.

Another object of Harris's zeal was smoking. He would snatch cigars or cigarettes from men's mouths and toss them to the ground. He opposed wake-keeping as well, and when the wife of Brand, the dispenser, died, he came in the morning to the house where she lay in state wearing her gold trinkets, surrounded by her friends. He ordered that the gold be taken off, the body put in the coffin, and that the burial should take place immediately, at noon. Brand, backed by Butler, refused to obey these orders. Harris in a rage cursed the whole company and withdrew. He must have realised that, in ordering burial at such a time, he was in effect accusing the woman of witchcraft or sorcery and of causing the death of her victims, for only those dying while practising some diabolical scheme were buried at midday. The point of this was to ensure that the wicked spirit, which could not come out during daylight, was buried and could no longer harm people, for a spirit which had escaped was even worse than one whose host was living.[25]

Although in the particular case cited above, Harris seems to have seized on a bad moment to lay down his rule, his commands as general pointers towards humane and civilised behaviour were sensible and enlightened. To suggest that funerals should not be long drawn out, extravagant and wasteful, that women should not be ostracised and penalised at a certain time of month, and to proclaim the desirability of cleanliness and of education, was to throw his strength behind the forces of progress.

Harris also forbade the pouring of libations and sacrifices, but the Omanhene had to continue with these rites as part of his official duty.

25. Explained by Canon C. H. Elliott, Cape Coast, in letter of 8 Nov. 1965

The Prophet Harris's impact on Axim cannot be gauged completely without reference to the influence on him of the well-known 'Fanti politician, Casely Hayford. Unfortunately, none of Hayford's personal papers relating to the period appears to have survived, so it is in his published works that we have to look for the evidence.

Joseph Ephraim Casely Hayford was one of several gifted sons[26] of that Rev. Joseph DeGraft Hayford who was prominent in the formation of the Fanti Confederation after 1867. Casely Hayford received the best education available in those days, attending the Wesleyan Boys' High School at Cape Coast and Fourah Bay College, before going on to Peterhouse, Cambridge, and the Inner Temple. He was called to the bar on 17 November 1896, and thereafter practised in several of the Gold Coast towns. During June 1914 he was evidently in his Axim chambers and thus able to observe the whole nature of the Apollonian mass movement.

Until 1914, and even a few years later perhaps, he thought politically in terms of a return to the past. This was natural in the son of his father and the nephew of Prince James Hutton Brew of Abura Dunkwa, leader of Fanti nationalism until his death in 1900. From 1916, Hayford was a Member of the Legislative Council of the Gold Coast, which suggests a changed attitude, and certainly by 1920, when he helped form the Congress of British West Africa, he was no longer aiming at putting the clock back, but rather at the fullest participation by Africans in British institutions imposed upon them and thus at the evolution of national independence.

In 1911 Casely Hayford published *Ethiopia Unbound: studies in race emancipation*, a collection of philosophical and religious speculations held together by a thin plot, which reveals a great deal about the author. The hero, Kwamankra, is descended from James Hayford, 'a good missionary', who one time served as British resident at Kumasi. Scion of an ancient Fanti house, educated in England, contemptuous of the African semi-educated professional classes who aped the European without understanding him, Kwamankra determines 'to devote the rest of his life in bringing back his people to their primitive simplicity and faith'.[27] Kwamankra is, in fact, an idealised projection of Casely Hayford, and his declared mission must be assumed to have been the latter's dream around 1910.

In the light of declarations in *Ethiopia Unbound*, it seems clear that when in June 1914 the Prophet Harris burst upon his sight, Hayford saw him as an ally. Harris, it seemed, was drawing strength from the depth of the

26. The Rev. J. DeGraft Hayford of Anomabue and his wife, Mary Brew, were the parents of three distinguished men in their generation: Dr Ernest J. Hayford (1858–1913), the Rev. Mark C. Hayford (1864–1935), and J. E. Casely Hayford (1866–1930).
27. Casely Hayford, *Ethiopia Unbound*, p. 75

spiritual heritage of Africa, but refining it by a marriage with European religious ideas to form a new and exciting synthesis leading to a new Africa. Although Hayford had always been a Methodist, it was rumoured in Axim that he was baptised by Harris, and he was noticeably active in reconciling the conservative Methodist congregation to an acceptance of the Prophet.

The little book he wrote day by day as he observed Harris at work was published in 1915 and gave the world in general its first intimation of marvels afoot in West Africa.[28] The writing is emotive: Hayford felt awe and admiration of Harris, and was apparently confident that something great was being born in the market place at Axim. 'He is a dynamic force of a rare order. He will move this age in a way few have done.' It could only have been from personal experience that he wrote: 'You come to him with a heart full of bitterness, and when he has finished with you all the bitterness is gone out of your soul.' On the same theme was: '"Miracles?" asks one sneeringly. It is not necessary to label the works of William Waddy Harris. But to me it is a greater miracle to drive bitterness out of one's soul than to calm physical agony. It is a miracle of miracles to turn God-ward the heart's aspirations.'

Surely the bitterness in his soul resulted from seeing incompetent and uninterested colonial officials ignoring the claims to equality and responsibility made by Africans like himself.[29] In *Ethiopia Unbound* he had written of his vision of the unspoilt African leading the world to regeneration. It happened after he had accompanied Dr Blyden, who happened to be in London at the same time, to an exhibition at the Royal Academy. They came to a painting of a wolf and a lamb living together, and Dr Blyden said, 'And a little child shall lead them—that is Africa'. Hayford came to the conclusion that it was not the spoiled imitation European who could carry out this regeneration, but rather 'The unspoilt son of the tropics, nursed in a tropical atmosphere, favourable to the growth of national life, he it is who may show us the way.'

In Harris he seemed to have found his unspoilt son of the tropics:

William Waddy Harris is strong on truth. All great personalities are strong on truth. They insist upon it. It is that which distinguishes them from the vulgar crowd whose fetish is cant. The soul of man was meant to be transparent. It was also meant to be clean. Convention and cant have covered it with mud. They have darkened it out of recognition. The sin of the age is insincerity.

28. Casely Hayford, *William Waddy Harris*
29. Casely Hayford, *Ethiopia Unbound*, p. 75ff describes such feelings for certain European government officers, including a colonial chaplain.

And with that, Harris gave his great message: '"Man, be yourself. It is no good mocking and deceiving yourself . . . truth, like humility, is an essential."'[30]

Then, of Harris's spiritual power he wrote:

> The soul of William Waddy Harris moves in the higher plane. . . . It seems as if God made the soul of Harris a soul of fire. You cannot be in his presence for long without realising that you are in contact with a great personality. He began as a reformer in the state. He ended as a reformer in the spiritual realm.

No longer advocating political rebellion against the Liberian authorities, Harris still used the term 'rebellion' constantly, denouncing authorities and powers without fear when they forced men to commit sins against God's Law, such as working on the Sabbath. His outspokenness was a sign not only of his courage but of his childlike simplicity:

> William Waddy Harris is a simple man. He wears a loose calico gown with a black tape thrown over and a rough woven cloth of the same material round his neck. He goes barefoot. He has tramped many a weary mile in search of souls. Humanity is fine when it is simple. It is simple when it is young. It is simple also in old age. Those whom the gods would specially bless they bring to a ripe old age, so that they may get a touch of simplicity before the last. William Waddy Harris is neither a child, nor a man bowed down in years. But he is a simple man. This, too, is of God. For God has humbled him.

Casely Hayford was impressed too by the humility Harris so often expressed.

> He says of the Christ that he took the form of a babe in order that by his helplessness he might indicate the true nature of humility. He reminds you that the Kroo man is the scavenger of the world. . . . Mammon has used the Kroo man all these years. And now God has need of him . . . God is using him now in the person of William Waddy Harris.[31]

If we based our final verdict on the writings of Casely Hayford we should be satisfied that their relationship was one in which a sophisticated man of the world sat at the feet of an inspired messenger whose holy

---

30. Casely Hayford, *William Waddy Harris*, p. 14. There is an echo here of words Hayford quoted from Dr Blyden, whose influence over the 'thinking youth of the race, lies in the fact that he has revealed in his writings and utterances the true motive power which shall carry the race on from victory unto victory . . . in one word "Man, know thyself".' This is found in Hayford's introduction to Blyden's *West Africa Before Europe*, p. iii.

31. *Ibid.*, p. 9

simplicity overwhelmed all base nature. The truth is not as straightforward as that. Casely Hayford not only learned from Harris, but his dialogue with him probably turned the Prophet's mind into new channels. Some observers believed that the revelations he received from Gabriel during his time at Axim were affected by outside suggestion. Father Stauffer, the missionary who disliked Hayford, wrote: 'The prophet, left to himself, would have done a lot of good. He did some good but would have done a lot more if some people had not been taking upon themselves the role of the Angel towards him.' He gives an example. A week or two after Harris's arrival in town, Casely Hayford told him that people could not understand why the Roman Catholic priest and the Wesleyan reverend had not yet come to pay their respects to the man who had brought so many converts to their churches. Harris replied. 'You have nothing to tell me. It is the Angel Gabriel alone who does command me.' That night the Angel spoke and the next day, said Father Stauffer, Harris talked and acted 'according to the suggestions of those black angels'. In the market-place he spoke of the priest and the minister and said: 'You will see what will happen if they do not come and do me homage.' Bruce (according to the Father) sent the Prophet a sack of rice, several fowls, and an invitation to dinner. Father Stauffer contented himself with sending the message that he was willing to get the Prophet free quarters and free food from the Government. That is, to have him put in prison. He had no further trouble until shortly before the Prophet turned his back on Axim, and this too involved Casely Hayford.

There was in Axim a group of young Fantis and mulattoes of somewhat superior education, employed in the firms or in business of some sort for themselves. Some of these men at first watched Harris from a distance mockingly, but later met at the house where he had been lodged (by the Omanhene) and conversed rather banteringly, from their superior position with the Prophet. These were the 'black angels' of Father Stauffer. Casely Hayford was the senior (then aged about forty-eight, not far short of Harris himself) and much the most influential of the group. The others included George Hutchful (a husband of Hayford's niece), Charles Grant (whose brother George was the most important African capitalist in the area), Ankuman Yanney, W. L. Phillips, and two brothers, E. B. Ephson and J. P. Ephson, from Elmina. Harris spoke freely to these men in English which verged at times on pidgin, though usually he rose above that.

An example of their mocking approach was when they asked Harris how it was that he who had come to Axim with two wives now had the company of five—how could he have more than one?

'There's no harm in that!' he cried, 'unless you take her to the altar. Even if you have a lawfully (i.e., church) married wife I will show you the way out of it. Tell her, I have seen this woman and I wish to marry her. If she refuses to agree, call a woman messenger to deliver exactly the same message. If she refuses again, call a second messenger and send the message again. Then it doesn't matter what she says, because you have told her in the name of Father, Son, and Holy Ghost.'

Another explanation of this is recorded by Father Stauffer, who claimed that Harris had arrived with one wife but his 'black angels' had put it to him that they, being 'big men', were surely not bound to one wife as poor men were. That was God's law for the white man, but did it apply to the black? Harris assured them that he could say nothing about it, the Angel would speak. That night came the revelation and next day it was publicly preached: 'God did not intend to make the same law for black and white people. Blacks could take as many wives as they could look after.'[33] The Prophet then took as his wives several women including Grace Thannie,[34] who were fetish priestesses won over by him. Whichever version of the story is more accurate, it is certainly true that henceforth Harris did not preach against polygamy.

Because of the scarcity of food (caused by the congestion of people at Axim, and the neglected farms), increasing sanitary difficulties, and the impossibility of having ships loaded on Sunday, the authorities were anxious to have Harris move on. The District Commissioner reprimanded him strongly. Harris, it is said, bore himself confidently, being sure of his authority from God and the power it gave him, and said, 'Ha! You are not pleased. Well, I leave Axim town and you will see.' So on a Sunday morning he and his wives started off for Sekondi. When the chiefs and people at Axim understood what was afoot, they brought him back, and for another fortnight he continued in the town.

Harris had been saying that he would go on to Sekondi and then 'through the instrumentality of the railway' to Kumasi. Explanations as to why he turned back at this point are various. Hayford wrote of him as saying, 'I received a message that I must leave this place. I must turn back. I am not to go forward. If I go to Seccondee, the people there will not hear.' He went on to say that the white people there would not listen to him and would work on Sunday. Therefore, God would plague them, white and black, until they were ready to listen. But it was not he, Harris, who would preach to them.

32. J. P. Ephson
33. Father Stauffer's Journal. He was wrong in saying Harris came with one woman; he came with two, and while he may have added three, it seems that only Grace Thannie joined him permanently.
34. Grace Thannie is honoured today as foundress of the Church of the Twelve Apostles (see below Chapter Eleven). She had been a fetish priestess at Eikwe Kristan.

Father Stauffer tells a rather different story, one in which he plays a leading role. Although, he says, the officials wished Harris would go away, they did not know how to effect his departure quietly. It was 'the black angels' who hastened his retreat, though that was not their intent. It hurt this group that Harris was welcome only in the Methodist Church. They asked him whether he was afraid of the Father. That night the Archangel spoke again, and next morning, Saturday, 25 July 1914, 'the black cherubs' came to announce to the Father that Harris would come next morning to preach in his church. Friends had already told Father Stauffer of the message being brought, and he refused to receive the delegation. They refused to leave, however, and at last he came out on the raised veranda of the Mission House where Casely Hayford, as spokesman, addressed him. The African lawyer opened fire first. 'What do you think of the Prophet?' Father Stauffer replied that Harris had at first done a lot of good and had brought many people to church but now, misled by 'some of you', he was doing wrong, teaching polygamy and inciting to revolt. Hayford abruptly delivered his message: 'The Prophet is coming to preach in your church tomorrow!' Stauffer answered: 'How dare you, a lawyer, educated in Europe, the brother of a Reverend, bring me such a message that a Krooman is going to preach in the Catholic Church when you know that nobody who is neither bishop nor priest, not even the Governor, is allowed to preach in a Catholic Church!'

Half an hour later the Prophet himself appeared on the veranda with a crowd of people. He told the priest: 'I tell you, you have to send away all the people who I brought to you. I am going to make my own church.' 'There are the stairs,' said Father Stauffer, gesturing with his hand. It took Harris a moment to understand his meaning, then, in great haste, he went, and according to the priest, left the town and headed back to the Ivory Coast.[35] If true, it indicates that Harris was baffled by a self-assurance which, because it would not bow before him, he had no way of overcoming.

Before the Prophet left Axim he pronounced a curse on the Catholic Church and those who worshipped there, incited perhaps by some of the Protestants. The next morning the new converts, fearful of death, stayed away from Mass. At the service Father Stauffer asked, 'who is the Prophet Harris?' and gave this answer, 'He is a liar.' He pointed out that whereas Father Fischer had been said to be stricken with blindness, he had since been seen in Axim perfectly healthy, and whereas Harris had at first spoken highly of the Catholic Church, he now said the contrary. 'Let everyone come to church without fear,' said the Father, 'they will not die.' That

35. Father Stauffer's Journal

Sunday there was a large Catholic funeral and the same night a candle-light procession through the streets. There were no deaths and on the next Sunday attendance was good again.

According to the Father, Harris soon reversed his attitude. A few days after leaving Axim he was again, at Essiama, asked to curse the local Catholic Church and said, 'the Father had done right. I am a prophet. I have to preach in the streets, not in the churches. It is Hayford—Hayford who has deceived me. Also the Catholics know the cross, they serve Christ; the Wesleyans do not know the cross, they do not know Christ.' This quotation may have been a product of wishful thinking by Father Stauffer's informant, or it may have been well-founded, for Harris was capable of sudden changes of mood which led him to be sometimes prudent in speech, sometimes unnecessarily provocative.

After Harris went away from Axim, fear kept his converts obedient to his teachings, and as he had warned that death would overtake those who broke his laws, the deaths which did occur were looked upon as indicative of guilt. A case in point was the woman described by a news correspondent thus: 'A certain woman who committed immorality after holding Professor Harris' Cross died last week and confessed on her dying bed the cause of her death. This will be a check to our female sex in Apollonia and other places.'[36]

When leaving, Harris warned the Omanhene: 'Your people I have healed, if they return to bad medicine, will die a foolish death—because in about four years a big sickness will come to the world.' Perhaps the last phrase was added after the flu epidemic of 1918.

On his way back he met many people who were pursuing him from the Ivory Coast, including many of the Sanwi Agnis. They had brought money for him, but he said he had enough to see him back to Liberia, and refused it. He also refused a proffered bag of rice.

The belated and only praise the Prophet received from Gold Coast officials was in connection with their attempts to introduce town-planning and public cleanliness in the coastal towns. The District Commissioner wrote: 'The sanitation of the villages between Half Assinie and Ancobra Mouth improved to a truly amazing degree during 1914. This is largely the work of the "prophet" as he was called.' After mentioning that he baptised and persuaded people to give up their jujus and go to church, the report concluded: 'He impressed upon them also that next to Godliness is cleanliness.'[37] The Provincial Commissioner, in a letter some nine months after Harris had withdrawn, wrote: 'Apollonia before Harris [*sic*] visit was steeped in fetishism and the towns and villages were in a most un-

36. *The Gold Coast Leader*, 12 Sept. 1914
37. Axim Record Book

Methodist church, Orbaff (with towers), photographed 1964

A reception in the compound of an Attié village chief, Ivory Coast, to welcome missionaries: seated (l. to r.) village catechist, Dr. W. J. Platt and M. Lethel

Translating the Bible into Adjoukrou by Methodist ministers: (l. to r.) D. H. Loko, J. B. Lawson, L. T. Balmer, E. K. Gata and A. D. Dickson

sanitary condition. All this has now been changed, places of worship and schools are to be found in every village, and the villages and towns are being remodelled on sanitary lines.'

Behind him, as he quit Apollonia, Harris left the two churches trying to cope with thousands[38] of former fetish practitioners battering their doors in an effort to become full-fledged Christians and thus be safe from the malevolent spirits Harris had driven away. The churches, for the most part, failed, but that is another chapter.

38. Armstrong, p. 38, speaks of 8000 people trying to join the Methodist Church.

CHAPTER SEVEN

Ivory Coast Triumph

THE FIRST SWIFT PASSAGE of Harris through the Ivory Coast virtually coincided with a strong effort on the part of the colonial Administration to transform the native population into productive, economically secure and tax-paying workers. We have already cited evidence for this (Chapter 6) and efforts seem to have been intensified early in 1914, judging by official reports. Those for the Cercle des Lagunes alone show the many influences active officials were bringing to bear. In January the inhabitants of Abidjan Rural were lectured on hygiene, public health, and the cleanliness of their huts and villages, and heard the accustomed exhortation to make new plantations of cash crops.[1] The Chef de Poste at Dabou, on his visits through Adjoukrou country in January, Abidji country in February, and along the Alladian coast in March and April, gave each group advice on the growing and harvesting of their cash crops. Where the Adjoukrous had collective oil palm plantations, as at Toupa, Débrimou, and Douboury, he gave instructions on the correct preparation of the oil to bring the best price. As a result the firms reported that impurities in the oil brought to them dropped from 15 per cent to 2 per cent in four months. The tax around Dabou and Abidjan was paid so promptly in January 1914 that it was cited by the officials as proof of the increasing wealth of the inhabitants.

The Abidjis had just begun, at this time, to take an interest in palms and were being encouraged to carry the oil along the new road built by their forced labour to the trading factories on the Ebrié Lagoon. They had kola-nut trees which they had never tried to utilise commercially, and the visiting Chef de Poste pointed out that these were a valuable commodity

1. Abid. X-46-25, Report of Chef de Poste, Abidjan Rural, Jan. 1914

which, if harvested, would fetch them good money. On the same visit he showed them how to grow cocoa and promised to send them 4000 plants for the beginning of March.

On the sandy Alladian coast, where hundreds of coconut palms grow, the natives were shown how to care for the palms which, they were told, could yield them a good income, and how to prepare copra. Until then they had been ignorant of the commercial possibilities of their coconuts. Already, in the stretch of coast between Adjué and Jacqueville, the possibilities of kola-nuts were being realised, and the Chef de Poste noticed many small trees being tended; only a short time before 'the Dioulas, Hausas, or Bambaras, the peddlers who went through the region,' had been the only ones to value this produce.

Everywhere in the subdivision of Dabou, cocoa plants were demanded by the Chiefs, new plantations were set out, and developed under the watchful eye of the Chef de Poste. In June some villages were discovered weeding their oil palm plantations of their own volition, having learned that this was essential for obtaining a good harvest. Only the year before it would have been almost impossible to get them to see the necessity; in 1914 at least one village did see it, and its example was so infectious that surrounding villages began to do the same.

In contrast to the people around the Lagoon, the forest people around Agboville, 'pacified' in 1909 and 1910, were in 1914 progressing very slowly towards civilisation, as the officials saw it. The reports of the Chef de Poste indicate his frustration. Early in the year he wrote:

> Although finally and steadily entered on the way of labour, the Abbey still needs to be supported, directed, and even stimulated in his first efforts. The Abbey region, exceptionally favoured by Nature, is a source of varied riches. But the native can satisfy his own needs without making the least effort to derive a profit. We cannot and ought not to ignore this inutilisation of resources, and we shall know better than to be satisfied with a feeble native exploitation. Therefore we ought to apply to the Abbeys, in the widest sense, the economic politics of obligation. Our duty is to push the natives without bullying or coercion, but with a tenacious patience, towards the intensive and rational exploitation of the wealth of the region.[2]

The Chef de Poste felt rewarded for his pressure on people to weed their plantations when the oil palm harvest amounted to 29 tons in 1914, compared with 6 tons the year before. During June and July, however, villagers were discovered stealing away to *campements* in the forest, and

2. Abid. X-46-25, Report of Chef de Poste, Agboville, Feb. 1914

when seeking out these and destroying them the Chef de Poste dis-covered, lurking in the depths of the forest, an old chief who had never surrendered after the 1910 rebellion and was encouraging hostility to the French in the villages around.[3]

These examples illustrate the clear-cut nature of the cultural confrontation taking place in these regions by 1913 and 1914. The situation was one in which old standards, practices and beliefs seemed to have lost their ability to guarantee stability and peace of mind, and men were searching for more satisfactory spiritual guides and guardians than those they knew. For this reason the French officials had actually been helped in some places to destroy the shrines of powerful spirits (p. 103). But they had not been able to offer an appealing new supernatural presence, and for this reason their reforms were sporadic and abortive of constructive consequences.

This was a perfect environment for William Wade Harris's prophetic mission. All that was needed was a sufficient expression of interest to circulate his fame over a wide area, and the general craving for spiritual certainty would bring people to him. The unparalleled success of his return visit to the Ivory Coast must have owed a great deal to rumours from Apollonia. It owed a great deal, also, to the work of the clerks, Brown, Goodman and others, far away in the Lahou area. Probably it took months for knowledge of the passage of Harris and the work being continued in his name to percolate through the inland populations, and longer still for them to act upon it. By July 1914 the Chef de Poste at Dabou (on the mainland) reported that a great number of Alladians, mostly chiefs and elders, had been travelling to a spot near Fresco to see a 'messenger of God' entrusted with a new religion for them. Such a messenger at this date can only have been one of the clerks at Ebonou, probably Brown. The pilgrims, returning home, burned their fetishes and constructed huts for prayer.

As the rumours of Harris's greatness trickled back from the Gold Coast to reinforce the belief in his miraculous achievements already held by some people along the Alladian Coast and at Grand Bassam, the indifference of many who had met or heard of the Prophet turned to keen interest. Oral tradition at Addah, an important Alladian village midway between Grand Lahou and Jacqueville, recounts that Harris on his first passage stayed one night there. During the evening he called the old men together and told them that the fetishes they feared were not gods; they should burn them and go to Brown at Ebonou to be baptised. The old men were not convinced, so he simply said, 'Well, I am going on my way. There is no pressure on you, but your hearts will lead you to do what I have said.'

3. *Ibid.*, July 1914

After he had gone, these *chefs de famille* discussed what he had said among themselves and with their wives and children, and reflected. It was true, they decided, and bit by bit, household by household, they began to burn their fetishes and make their way to Brown at Ebonou. Deputations from other villages acted in the same way, and found not only Brown but, closer at hand, his deputy at Grand Lahou. This man was known to them simply as 'Papa'. It is certain that many of the thousands later said to have been baptised at Lahou by Harris were actually baptised by Brown and 'Papa'.

When Victor Nivri, the *chef de canton*, a Catholic, saw the mobs of Alladians, Adjoukrous, and Ebriés passing through Addah en route to Lahou, he decided, after consulting his elders, to seek power needed to baptise people himself. He was carried by hammock to Grand Lahou where 'Papa' regretted that he had no authority to delegate power. Nivri went on to Brown, who received him, instructed him for two weeks, and gave him full authority to baptise.

From that time Addah became a centre for pilgrimage, and Nivri even made trips to other villages to administer the rite. Some of the people he baptised came from Adjué, another large Alladian village further east. Harris, on his first passage, had spent one night here, at the house of Njako the Chief. Adjué had a unique fetish object (probably a large metal cylinder) which had been bought from the English traders and enshrined under the name of Kragbin N'Je, complete with a Chief Priest and assistants. This Priest and other elders were summoned to meet Harris. When they heard from him that God, the Creator, did not like fetishes to be worshipped, they scorned his message and rejected him as a madman. They told him that they were not able to drive the fetish spirits away (evidently they did not realise that Harris claimed the power to do that himself) and the Prophet, enraged, stalked from the village and continued eastwards. No voice was raised in his support. The *féticheurs*, however, changed their minds. A whirlwind blew through the town the same afternoon and while it did not do much damage (rumour much exaggerated its effect, as it was reported in other places) it was sufficiently obvious as a sign to lead to second thoughts about Harris. From that time on, they began to burn their fetish objects and went to Lahou or, later, to Addah, to be baptised.

At some time after Nivri took up the work, a large number of the inhabitants of Mopoyeme, a sizable town of Adjoukrous on the inner side of the lagoon, near Dabou, were baptised by him. Their experience was typical of many from across the lagoon. The news had reached them that God had sent someone to baptise all who agreed to burn the fetishes and to cease to worship the fetish spirits. The 'baptism' signified something new, something important, that they had never known of before. They sent six young persons to Lahou to investigate. There they found only 'Papa', a Sierra Leonean, who baptised them and gave them Harris's commands. On their return, they persuaded the rest of the villagers to burn their fetishes and seek baptism. The old Priest of the village was dead and they had not chosen a new guardian for the village shrine from among the eligible old men, so they burned its contents along with their own fetish objects and set out by canoe for Addah, which was closer than Lahou.

On arrival at the village they went directly to Victor Nivri's house. He asked why they had come. They said they had heard that he would baptise them, and that they wished to worship God. He fetched his Bible and, when he was sure that they had burned their fetishes, he read to them from it and told them what they must do to merit admittance to Heaven. He then dismissed them for that day. Next morning, when the church bell had sounded, the men and women seated themselves, in separate groups, in the village square. Nivri announced that it was time for the baptism; if they were attached to the Devil they must break with him *now*! If they had not burned their fetishes they must do so before they entered their homes again. Nivri was dressed for the ceremony in a white robe with a white turban, and he carried a large dish of water and a cross of sticks. There were people from many villages there, and he baptised each in the name of the Trinity. Some, he thought as he came to them, were attracted to the Devil and he made the sign of the cross before their eyes. People who were given to witchcraft cried out in agitation. Two of the villagers were especially agitated; a man thrashed his head and limbs about and a woman completely lost control of her excretory functions and was a pitiful sight.

When the group from Mopoyeme returned home, they followed Nivri's instructions and built a church for prayer, looking for guidance to a young man, Moise Lat, who had been appointed *Predicateur* or preacher when he visited Lahou. He turned out to be so lacking in initiative that they replaced him by Djedjre who had also gone to Lahou and who, furthermore, spoke some English. Lat was given another official post, that of bell-ringer.[4]

In August, when the Chef de Poste from Dabou toured the coastal areas of his district, he found fetishes burnt, churches built, and the people everywhere practising what he called 'Protestantism'. He noticed two excellent effects of this sudden conversion: that since the destruction of the fetishes, a great many young men had returned to the villages they

4. Oral evidence of old men at Mopoyeme, Aug. 1964

had left because they were afraid of being poisoned, and that every day, save Sunday, was devoted to labour.[5] At Jacqueville the officer found, in mid-August, many Abidjis and Adjoukrous. He evidently did not connect them with the new faith, and ordered them home, warning them not to return without passes.

During August 1914, while war clouds gathered over Europe and all local Frenchmen, even the missionaries, were considering how mobilisation would affect them, trade in the Ivory Coast came almost to a standstill. It was not the European situation which directly caused this, but the fact that the firms were refusing to accept manillas (small copper or brass bars, often bent into a horse shoe shape, which had been an acceptable currency in many parts of West Africa since the sixteenth century) as a medium of exchange, while the producers felt they were not being offered a fair price for their produce and held it back. The foreign peddlers, who usually acted as middlemen, had drifted away. From the administraion's point of view, this was one good result.

The Chef de Poste at Dabou guarded against a new kind of exploitation, by instructing each village that their pastor must be presented to him before installation. During September the mainland villages of the Adjoukrous and Abidjis were discovered to be equally given over to the new faith. They were no longer observing the taboos which prevented them from labouring a full six days. During September 'a provocative pastor', presumably the clerk known as 'Sam', moved from Lahou to Jacqueville where he baptised numerous Alladians, then came to Bouboury, where many Adjoukrous went to him. The Chef de Poste understood that the leading figures of Débrimou and Orbaff had sent an invitation to the great pastor at Lahou, 'Jesus Christ', and the Chief of Débrimou, Albert Katakre, said he would be with them in the early part of October. Since the disciple who came was universally known as 'Papa', it would seem that the officer had badly misunderstood the Chief, as well as the nature of Papa's teaching. He did know that the pseudo-Jesus Christ forbade the drinking of too much alcohol, and recommended work for six days and rest on Sunday, and since these teachings were excellent, he would not interfere with the man but would watch him discreetly.[6]

While his message was being preached by the clerks, Harris was on his way back to the Ivory Coast, and he must have been surprised at the enthusiastic welcome, after the comparative indifference he had met a few months before. Cécaldi, the Administrateur at Bassam, had died, a few

5. Abid. X-46-25, Report of Chef de Poste, Dabou, Aug. 1914
6. *Ibid.*, Sept. 1914

days after Harris had left the town, and since he had quarrelled with the official and was said to have predicted the death,[7] there was no doubting his power and that of his God.

Moreover, many Ivoirians had heard of his power from the Apollonians and Agnis who had gone to the Gold Coast to find him. On his return to Assinie, the inhabitants of inland parts of the Cercle came down *en masse*, even the notables from Krinjabo, the capital of the old Sanwi kingdom. Harris baptised them and made his only known effort to establish an independent church. He laid hands on John Swatson, the Methodist agent at Aboisso, and sanctified him as 'Bishop of Sanwi'. Swatson was to carry on the evangelisation of the hinterland, for Harris was steadfast in his intention to stay close to the coast and would not even go up to visit Krinjabo or Aboisso.

At Assinie he met a delegation from Bonoua, the chief centre of the Abouré-Akapless tribe which lived inland from the coast along the lower reaches of the Comoé River. The four men begged Harris in the name of their chief, Anoh Andouké, to come and destroy their fetishes. He promised to visit Bonoua when he had finished at Assinie. Perhaps he forgot, or followed a sudden whim, as he was prone to do, for instead of going to Bonoua, he went to Bassam. There, enthusiastic throngs demanded that he put on their heads the water of God that he carried with him.

BINGERVILLE

At Bingerville, the capital, Governor Angoulvant learned with interest of the return of the Prophet, known to him by rumour. At his command Harris was brought to his palace, and, after a meeting of the two men, the Governor asked the acting Superior of the Catholic Mission, Father Gorju, to talk to him. Although Father Gorju later attacked Harris with immoderate venom, the Prophet's charm made a favourable impression on them at their meetings, and as Harris attended mass and encouraged his converts to do the same, the Church saw no reason to condemn him. Angoulvant went further and publicly expressed his approval of the Prophet's teachings when he met the indigenous population during tours of inspection, for 'seeing that he preached obedience to the Administration's authority, forbade the misuse of alcohol and converted the *féticheurs* who had been, for a long time, the causes of revolt against the French, the Government of the Ivory Coast judged his presence as being of great service to all'.[8] Years later, when the Governor was asked about Harris, he remembered him as a hypnotist whose powers were used for

7. Hartz, 'Le Prophète Harris', p. 120
8. Amon-d'Aby, *La Côte d'Ivoire dans la cité africaine*, p. 152

purposes beyond reproach and whose teachings offended the Administration in no way.[9]

The Chef de Poste at Abidjan concurred in the approval of Harris's teachings, though he did not believe that Harris's role as 'prophet' was understood in more than a confused way. They acclaimed him largely 'because he brought a new religion', an observation of greater significance than the official intended. Converts informed him that they were commended to live on good terms with the white men (presumably the officials), to earn their living by six days of hard work followed by a Sunday consecrated to prayers and complete rest. The officials were happiest about the destruction of the fetishes. The Chef de Poste wrote: 'The Administration can only rejoice about it provided that the propagation of this religion . . . works for the good of civilisation.'

In oral tradition among the Harris converts, his weeks spent in the vicinity of Bingerville are recalled as a time of marvels. Housed by Kofi Justin, an official interpreter, he lived in the shadow of the gubernatorial palace and there summoned first the townspeople. They were hostile; some of them had come intending to kill him (supernaturally, one presumes) and asked him at once, 'You, with what power and for what reason do you come here?' Harris felt that only a miracle would convince them that he had power, so he and the women sang a hymn, then he thrust his staff up towards the sky, pointing to the sun. The sun whirled about in a circle, and then a little black cloud grew overhead and from it rain fell on the wicked people. It did not rain on the good people standing beside him. When the rain had stopped, Harris said, 'What do you want now?' 'To be baptised,' they answered. Harris replied, 'I have baptised you with the rain,'[10] which would appear to have disappointed the people, who had intended him no harm. Despite that touch to heighten the mystery, it seems likely that the rain fell on everyone and that all were considered baptised together.

Another story, possibly a different version of this, is told about the village of Akue Sauté, near Bingerville, which was rejecting Harris's baptism. He set out to visit them as soon as he heard of the villagers' opposition. When they refused to prepare for baptism, he called a torrential rainfall by pointing his staff at the sun. Then they repented of their bad conduct and told him so. With a gesture of his staff in the opposite direction, Harris brought the shower to an end, made the sun shine warmly, and went ahead baptising the people in his normal way.

It is an interesting corroboration of Harris's reputation as a rainmaker that he cited it as proof of his prophetic vocation when talking to Father

9. Bianquis, *Le Prophète Harris*, p. 11
10. Abraham Nandjui

Gorju, though he placed it second to his power to effect changes in the lives of the crowds who surrounded him and heard him preaching. He told the Father a number of things about his life in a way which shows that the Prophet controlled the man in him. When he received his call, he said, he was told that he must give up his wife as a sacrifice; thus he rationalised her death, which his children knew was caused by her grief when she realised that he had become 'mad' in prison. He told him that he was the Prophet come to announce the thousand years of peace spoken of by St John in the Book of Revelation Chapter 20.

The Superior of the Mission thought it was wrong of Harris to baptise (Father Gorju later wrote that the fact that this baptism was probably valid, at least in form, was 'not the least of our worries'). Harris replied that Christ had instructed him to baptise as a preservation against the influence of the fetishes the people had abandoned. 'This preservative, it is the water and the influence which the touching of my cross exerts upon them.'[11]Despite their approval of some of his results (not least of these the crowds now coming to church) the Fathers finally asked Harris to baptise no more. His answer was to bring some hundreds of people to the Mission for the Fathers to baptise. The latter said that instruction had to be given first, to make suppliants capable of grasping the virtue of baptism. Harris replied, 'God will do that.'

Although Harris was willing to cooperate with the Catholic Mission, it was not his intention or, perhaps, in his power, to force his converts to become Catholics against their will. About two kilometres from Bingerville was a village, Adjamé, which, like others, was hesitant about coming to Harris until the chief fetish priest and six others were baptised. The first reaction of the rest of the villagers was to try to kill the defaulters by sorcery, but when they failed, they all came to be baptised. Shortly after, Harris appeared in the centre of the village, accompanied by a Catholic Father, and told the people they must build a church in which to worship. The Priest said nothing, but the people suspected that he intended to take charge of the church. The missionaries had come to Adjamé before, telling the inhabitants to burn their fetishes, but when they had done so there were deaths, so they no longer trusted the power of the Fathers and their God.

They said to Harris, 'You, perhaps, are sent by God and we want to listen to you alone—don't turn us over to these people!' Harris heard them out sympathetically and promised that other white men, not the Fathers, would come to teach them about God. A few days later he asked a Fanti trader at Aboubou, whom the Ebriés knew as 'Krak', to come and teach the village to know God. Krak first showed Harris his Bible. Harris

11. Hartz, p. 122

approved it and told the villagers. 'The white men who are coming will bring this sort of Bible.'[12]Then he ordered Krak to teach them some new songs, and told them that whereas formerly they had danced in honour of the fetishes and sung praises to them, now they were to dance and sing praises to God. Krak then taught them Christian hymns and they danced to them.[13]

The man who became *chef d'église* (preacher) of the new church was the same chief priest who had led the first group to Bingerville. It becomes obvious from this account that when the leading intercessors with the spirits had publicly lost faith in the powers of those spirits, then the bulk of the people, who made no special claim to any intimacy with the spirit world, would find conformity with the new faith the path of least resistance.

During the weeks Harris spent at Bingerville, crowds of people came, not only from the immediate vicinity, but from far inland, as the rumour of his power spread; many of them believed that the government was particularly anxious to have them come to Harris and, in general, this was true.

As the news of the burning of fetish objects by Harris and his disciples spread during the third quarter of 1914, many more of the devotees of the spirits began to lose confidence in them. The story became current that the spirits were saying to their initiates that they were retiring to a distant place, ceding their territory to the new power which was coming. They were also reported as saying that they had been judged and were to be punished. Since the spirits had thus abandoned their position, people saw no risk in burning the objects associated with them. The Ebriés, for example, understood that henceforth the one great god, Attoutou Yankan (or Attoutou Yankan-Yangoblessoué) would himself protect them from sickness and make them rich and numerous, though previously they had never visualised him as being concerned with the cares and joys of their little lives.

At Bingerville, groups of ten were baptised, all holding Harris's cross at once. He spoke the words of the baptism in English and they were translated as he did so, while he made the sign of the cross in water on their foreheads and touched their heads with his Bible. These last two actions made some people fall into convulsions. After each group was baptised, while a new group was coming forward, Harris and the three women sang hymns and shook their calabashes.

---

12. This would be the English King James Version and in so far as his converts believed that this version alone was valid, they would refuse the ministrations of the Catholic Fathers.
13. Oral evidence of Amos Ahin, Eugene Leloux, Emmanuel Gbedje, Alfred Banho, and Paul Kolan, old men in the Methodist Church at Adjamé-Bingerville, Aug. 1963

Harris is said to have been very agitated at such gatherings. His movements were often fast and he shouted loudly when he was displeased. Each day, when all had been baptised, he told them that his baptism rested on their repentance (presumably this meant it protected them only so long as they did not fall back into the sin of fetish worship), and that after him would come learned people to teach them about God and His works, and how to gain salvation. In the meantime, they were to build churches to honour the Eternal there.

The terror surrounding Harris and his God continued to increase. Those who tried to outwit them died, as Harris warned they would. According to a Sierra Leonean observer, a Mr Campbell, there was an example of this at Bingerville. He wrote:

We did not hear him say anything would happen which did not happen immediately or in the space of 24 hours. I was a witness once. When he baptised at Bingerville, a man took the road ... from Commerce, below Alepé, to come to Harris to be baptised—the prophet told him he had put to one side some of his favourite idols before coming and, because of that, he ought to return and burn them, for, if he were baptised, he could not return home, he would die in the road. The man denied that he had left any idol hidden before coming. He was baptised at Bingerville and left the same day, Monday, for his town of Commerce. I was then at the bank of the river Alepé where men who came from all parts left their boats to go to the towns. ... The man came to the edge of the river and some of his neighbours, who knew him, were with us ... and told us that in truth the man had left some fetishes concealed in the bush at home, when to our great surprise the man, having embarked in his boat, collapsed and died before our eyes.[14]

An important embassy, from Bonoua, caught Harris at an encampment called Hoflobou, on the seashore. They persuaded him that he must come to Bonoua by telling him of a wizard named Abbi who had claimed he could kill Harris by giving him some powdered tobacco. Harris could not resist the challenge.

The return to Bonoua led them over the Kodjoboué Lagoon, which had three taboos attached to it. Those crossing dared not say the name of a one-eyed man, or of an albino, and a woman in her period could not cross. The Bonoua men suggested that Harris should baptise the lagoon and dissolve these restrictions. He did so; he propelled himself over the water, lifted his staff and made a long prayer, and when he had finished a torrential rain fell, though the Prophet was still in the sunlight. They

14. Bianquis, p. 34

moved on to Bonoua, where they found that the *féticheur* Abbi had vanished.[15]

Gaston Joseph, writing close to the event, described the wizard as having been vanquished after a public confrontation. According to his account, the fetish priest, Labri (from Abidji country) declared that Harris (Latabou) could do nothing against his fetish, and even accepted two thousand francs from a group of villagers who wanted him to prevent Harris from coming. Evidently the village was split in its attitude to fetishes, as in 1904. When Harris did arrive, he found the *féticheur* dancing and gesticulating in front of the fetish hut, but on seeing Harris, his courage failed and he fled into the bush. The people gathered together, the fetishes were burned, and all, including a wife and nephew of the *féticheur*, were baptised.[16]

Those who were sick were cured on touching the cross. After baptising them Harris told the villagers that they should go either to the Protestant or to the Catholic Church. He said that messengers and evangelists would come to encourage the newly baptised and make them familiar with the Bible and the Holy Word in it. The Catholic Fathers thought the people would now come to them, as the power of the fetishes was broken, but the stumbling block for the villagers was that these priests would not permit polygamy.

THE MOMENTUM OF THE HARRIS MOVEMENT

The religious movement inspired by the Prophet Harris developed swiftly in several different ways after it was, in effect, licensed by Angoulvant. Firstly, there was the work Harris did himself; then there was the work of his designated or self-styled disciples; and, finally, there was the effect of the wave of rumour which swept inland, arousing expectations without giving a very clear understanding of what was happening on the coast.

Harris worked steadily to the end of the year, wandering from village to village near the coast, at first in the vicinity of Grand Bassam and later he remained at Kraffy. Strangely enough, although he was anxious to provide his Ebrié converts with instructors from among the clerks, he did not seek the aid of the Rev. H. G. Martin, who had just arrived as the first Protestant missionary to be stationed in the colony.

The clerks carried on the main burden of evangelisation and organisation of the converts. The Adjoukrous, for example, who accepted the new religion with great sincerity, for the most part never saw Harris himself. Few of them went to Kraffy; most of them were baptised in the

---

15. Jean Ekra
16. Joseph, *La Côte d'Ivoire*, p. 159

chief centres of their own country by the disciples Papa and Sam. A minority had probably sought baptism already, from Brown, Nivri, or Goodman, but the majority were unconverted at the time Harris was received at Bingerville. Since the disciples accomplished as much as Harris in changing the lives of the people and freeing them from the dead hand of traditional religion, Governor Angoulvant's theory that Harris was a hypnotist becomes quite irrelevant.

One group of Adjoukrous had been sent to meet Harris, during the first half of the year, from Bohnné, a village on the lagoon shore west of Dabou. It consisted of eleven people, one an epileptic youth, Nathaniel, who had been badly hurt by a fall from a palm tree, and a woman who suffered from sores all over her skin. The rest were not seeking to be healed but were persons of authority who wanted to test the Prophet's power. When they reached Grand Lahou, Harris was long since gone, but they found Sam and Papa working there as a team, with Papa carrying the water and Sam the Bible. They had no cross. Papa read from the Bible when he preached, and some of the Lahou people sang. When Nathaniel was baptised he began to shake, even after Papa made the sign of the cross in his face. After about an hour he felt something coming out and said to his friends, 'The sickness has left me'. Similarly, the woman was permanently cured.

When the eleven pilgrims returned home, the rest of the villagers wanted to be baptised and went to Victor Nivri at Addah. The village church was set up under Brim (who had been chief and priest of the village) and Metch, who had been among the first group of pilgrims to Papa and were chosen as preachers by him.

Débrimou was the Adjoukrou centre where most of the tribe were baptised, along with Ebriés, Attiés, and Abbeys, after Papa came over from Grand Lahou. This was apparently during the months of October and November, 1914. The infant Laurent Lassm, later to become head of the Ivory Coast Methodist Church, came with his family and the rest of the village of Youhouli. There were more than 5000 Adjoukrous gathered there, sheltered from the dry season sun by palm-frond pavilions. When a heavy shower unexpectedly fell, Papa did not use his basin of water but touched the heads the rain had wet and baptised them.

The Débrimou people had been ready for the new faith from the time they heard of Harris's arrival at Lahou, as 'Nyam-Etchi-Egm-Ek'rm' ('Message of God'). Those among them who had the ability to detect the presence of the spirits, said that these had fled and left the fetish objects, such as those attached to Séké (a protection against witches and death), Tano (a source of riches), Mando (a defence against devils),[17]

17. Mando became extremely popular in many regions about this time, and pushed more traditional spirits to the side.

and Diby (a defence against the evil of other people), as mere lumps of material substance. As Harris had instructed, the people began to work six days and rest on the seventh, and they waited and prayed for the coming of the white missionaries he was said to have promised.

It was apparently a Sierra Leonean trader, Jack Harris, who invited Sam to come to the Adjoukrou villages. He came to Mopoyeme, near the lagoon, where, like Papa at Débrimou, he spoke in English and had an interpreter. People from the interior, including Abidjis, were baptised by him there and later, after baptising at Bouboury, Pass, and other places, he set off inland into Abbey country. This was in defiance of the local Commandant who had told him on 21 November, when he found the people at Mopoyeme being taught to worship in English, that he should return to Lahou forthwith. On the very next day Sam was baptising at Pass. The Chef de Poste also told the people to sing their hymns and say their prayers in French. This evidently alarmed them, because they had bought an English Bible, which they were accustomed to open every Sunday in the church. There were some old men, too, who feared this Bible because of the magic in it, so the Preacher took it in a valise and gave it to Papa.

Sam had also visited Bouboury, where the people had already destroyed the fetishes in the assurance that God was more powerful. They felt a relief, because the fetishes were expensive protectors. Sam finished baptising them and they chose a preacher and twelve apostles for their church. Henceforth they kept the Sabbath by praying in the church, by resting from work, and by taking collections which were used to buy lights and a cloth for the table. They also obtained an English Bible and a church banner inscribed in English.

At Pass, also on the lagoon, the people were lucky enough to catch Harris at Kraffy. When they returned they broke their Mando and other idols, believing they were useless now that God had come, for the spirits had fled before Him. Otherwise the fetishes would have killed them when they paddled their canoes towards Kraffy. They believed Harris when he told them they would be struck by heavenly fire if they tried to worship the idols again. The villagers made a pavilion for their Sunday services, and on that day they sang and repeated the Prophet's words and respected all his prohibitions; they did not even dare walk in the bush, for if they were touched by a green leaf, it was a sin. As Harris had instructed them, they appointed twelve old men to be the 'twelve apostles', and the leader, the chef d'église, was known as the 'Peter' of the Church.[18]

Viewed as a whole, the Adjoukrou conversion was remarkably effective

18. Oral evidence of the Rev. Jean Mel, native of Pass, July 1963

and the reason for this was probably essentially the same in all the coastal villages: the conversion took place through the leaders of the community. The most powerful group in the Adjoukrou community were the active old men, the *Ebebou*, and these were the religious and secular leaders. They had the power to inflict evil and death or goodness and life, the spirits spoke through them to men, and men through them to the spirits. These were the men who knew most about spiritual power and fetishes and who, when they wilted before the power of Harris, had no alternative but to be persuaded by it and to become most ardent preachers of it. The rank and file followed them into this new faith, as they had formerly followed them into the cult of Mando and the old gods before him.

Just as the fetishes had ruled by terror, the new God was also believed to bring death or illness to those who disobeyed him. At Orbaff a man went to the bush on Sunday when he should have been at service. On his way home he fell dead in front of the church. This judgment kept the sanctity of the Sabbath inviolate.

On the other hand, the new faith offered some very real benefits. There was now the prospect of a happy eternal life, instead of an unsubstantial existence at some nearby 'village of the dead', and there was relief from the taboos which forbade work on many days and which prevented the consumption of many totem animals and fish.

At the end of October, the Governor was still giving his support to the Harris Movement. On a tour of inspection in the Dabou area, where he had to assure people that their manillas would be redeemed in silver, and to explain to them why France was at war, he also told them that he had given Harris permission to remain in the country. He was happy to see the good huts they were building for their churches, because they would soon have the opportunity of building similar ones for an instructor and dispenser whom he intended to send them.[19]

There was every reason for the Governor to be pleased. As in Apollonia, so in the most developed cercles of the Ivory Coast, among the Ebriés and Adjoukrous, the Abourés, the Abidjis, the Avikams and Aizis, the preachings of Harris were bringing about a revolution in thought and action. The change tended to make relations between officials and the Ivoirians easier and more constructive. In fact, Harris specifically told people to be obedient to the government.

In instructing people to believe in one God, to rest only on His day and work on the other six, Harris introduced the idea of regular labour which the French had been trying to inculcate. On this foundation of cooperativeness and a willingness to work regularly the efforts of the

19. Abid. X-46-25, Report of Chef de Poste, Dabou, Oct. 1914.

officials to introduce cash crops were reinforced. As long as the preaching of Harris and his assistants tended towards this outcome, there was no criticism to be made of him, and his reputation has rested, quite properly, on the amazing change he effected in the coastal regions of the Cercles de Lahou, des Lagunes, and de Bassam.

This movement was, briefly, a revitalisation of a sick society, a society which had lost faith in the power of the spirits it honoured and which feared the malevolence of wizards and witches. The demands of tradition, especially in the taboos which restricted freedom, were in direct conflict with the demands of the colonial power. Harris's new revelation banished the pressures from the traditional side and offered a leeway for adjusting to the administration's demands. Ordinary missionaries, lacking Harris's supernatural power, could not banish the witches, though perhaps being white-skinned they enjoyed a personal immunity from them. Harris, a black man, was a guarantee to other black men that they could become immune to spiritual harm. He could share his power to baptise to the clerks, who appeared to the people suffused in the glow of the Prophet's own charisma.

CHAPTER EIGHT

The Expulsion of Harris

FOR SOME MONTHS the Ivory Coast administration remained happy with their prophet and his constructive accomplishments, but gradually they began to fear that something was developing which they did not want and might not be able to control. Although they did not officially accuse Harris himself of fomenting trouble, they did become concerned about his imitators and helpers.

These preachers began to be noticed over a widespread area in October, and while some may never have been sent out by Harris, it was known that while in Bingerville he was commissioning English-speaking clerks (perhaps unemployed as a result of the dislocation of trade immediately following the outbreak of war) to go out and preach as his 'apostles'. The Chef de Poste took a very unfavourable view of this and thought these preachers should be watched carefully, for the greater number were not worthy of their office and had nothing to recommend them. The Governor, more sympathetic, suggested only that if any of these disciples were discovered robbing the people or otherwise committing crimes, they should be locked up. If not, they should be left at peace.

He did not realise that a third phase of the mass movement was taking place, beyond the area which Harris had visited himself. One such section was in the north of the Cercle des Lagunes. There, around Agboville, in the country of the Attiés and north of that, among the Abbeys and Agnis, religious excitement became noticeable only in October. These people were less accustomed to the European presence and the adjustments it required than were the lagoon peoples. They were in the area which Angoulvant had felt could not be pacified by peaceful means. At the beginning of his appointment he had announced his intention of really taming the independent Attiés and between 10 May and 13 June 1909 he had sent forces which brought them to heel. Their neighbours, the Abbeys, had armed themselves for the coming struggle and, led by their *féticheurs*, had broken the new railway line (which ran through their country) on 6 January 1910. They had derailed a train, cut telegraph lines, threatened Agboville, and rumours of the atrocious massacres they were said to have perpetrated terrified the towns. For nearly two weeks Agboville had been cut off, but with the arrival of reinforcements the Abbeys had been attacked in their villages until they surrendered in September 1910.

The course of the Harris movement among these three tribes was not the thorough-going spiritual revolution which took place on the coast. It was in October 1914 that the officials noticed that the natives were claiming to follow the teachings of the 'Son of God', as they called Hárris, but in fact, while they kept Sunday as a day of rest, this did not lead them to work the other six days. The rule which forbade the abuse of alcohol seemed to be little regarded, for in the special huts built for the new cult in all the villages were set open bottles of gin, such as had been found formerly in the fetish huts. [1] There were also in the area 'messengers of Harris', whether authorised or not, whom the Chef de Poste suspected of taking money from the people. Angoulvant, still convinced that the movement was beneficial, suggested that certain Fantis were causing the trouble and should be suppressed. As he commented on the margin of the official's report: 'Of course the Prophet Harris will have imitators less disinterested than himself, but it will be easy to send them before the tribunal of the subdivision at their first act of dishonesty.' [2]

These official reports tend to show that the point of Harris's preaching was lost on these inland peoples. To them he remained as he had been when the first rumour of his coming reached them, a 'great fetish', or a new god. Recent accounts from these three tribes bear out this interpretation.

On 12 November 1914 the Administrateur of the Cercle des Lagunes thought fit to put the Governor on guard with respect to the whole Harris movement. He cast no doubts on the sincerity of Harris himself, but thought the zeal of his disciples lay in the prospect of receiving goods from the faithful. He admitted that on this point Harris had been 'of a disinterestedness as remarkable as it is prudent, which alone has justified us in tolerating his presence in the colony'. However, he urged, if a close watch on them showed that the disciples were committing any dishonesty

1. Abid. X-46-25, Report of Chef de Poste, Agboville, Oct. 1914
2. *Ibid.*, comment on margin

in obtaining a fair remuneration for their priestly offices, they should certainly be brought before the tribunal of the subdivision.[3]

At the end of that month the Chef de Poste reported that the activity of the 'Son of God' was still being observed, although Harris himself had left the Cercle des Lagunes. While his actions were not obviously hostile to the French, the natives had become even more apathetic to the improvements the administration was trying to foster among them. For example, at the beginning of November they had been asked to fix that section of the Biassalé road stretching between Aboudé and Yaozrah, and they did it unwillingly. They were very busy at that time constructing churches.[4]

Furthermore, numerous emissaries of Harris had been, and were still, circulating in the region, baptising and extorting funds from the natives. It was very difficult to catch these individuals because the natives helped them to hide themselves.

It is certain that with the disappearance of Harris, this effervescence will diminish until, little by little, it will disappear completely. Within a few weeks a majority of the Abbeys will have already forgotten the Prophet, provided that his emissaries be energetically hounded and it be made impossible for them to carry on with their rogueries.

Along the coast, the new religion seemed solidly entrenched during November and the regions which had seen Harris himself were now, it was reported, 'plagued by false prophets' imitating him. Even in the Abidjan region, men from the English colonies and members of the Wesleyan Church were going into the Ebiré villages on Sundays, directing the services and instructing in the necessity for collections. Threatened with the tribunal, 'these false ministers' thereafter stayed at home.

In the interior, around Adzopé, the Attiés were, officials claimed, being converted to the new religion during October, and in November the Harris disciples were reported on every hand. From beyond the borders of this Cercle, in the Cercle du N'Zi-Comoé, there were similar reports. At the end of November the Chef de Poste at Bongouanou could write:

The approach of the 'son of God', as they call William Harris, has somewhat intrigued the *indigènes* who have immediately sent for the news. An emissary, on returning to his village Kangandissou, has made the place agog with excitement, and I would almost say with joy, by announcing that the Prophet was coming to expel all the whites and that his power was irresistible. He has been apprehended and disciplined, the population spoken to, and things have immediately been restored to normal.

3. Dakar, Report of Administrateur, Cercle des Lagunes, 12 Nov. 1914
4. Abid X-46-25, Report of Chef de Poste, Agboville, Nov. 1914

At Assié Akpoessé, on the other hand, the Chief has washed his stool and burned all the *fétiches* of the village, hence a great palaver with the chief of the tribe. The inhabitants of Assié Akpoessé were sure, according to the tidings brought back by their messengers from Agboville where Harris is said to be, that the latter would give them the power of being free and no longer ordered about by anybody.[5]

However, while these incidents interested him, the Chef de Poste saw nothing serious in them. The administration evidently felt otherwise, for this report was one of several sent on eventually to Dakar.

Meanwhile, in the regions along the Ebrié Lagoon, the Harris movement was pulsating and, even there, was beginning to cause concern to the administration. The Chef de Poste found Victor Nivri of Addah baptising villagers at some distance from home. 'I invited him to go exercise his ministry in his own village.'[6] At Mopoyeme he found 'Samuel' and warned him to go away. Harris himself was wandering somewhere along the coast between Assinie and Bassam.

During the months in which religious excitement swept the country the Fathers of Lyon hesitated to define their attitude towards it. At the beginning they had patronised Harris and were delighted with the crowds which overwhelmed their little church at Bingerville and demanded Holy Medals to wear as signs of their new allegiance. When, following mobilisation, the Fathers were reduced in numbers from about seventeen to six, they became alarmed at the strength of Harris's success. At the end of October they conferred and decided to watch carefully the results of 'the magnetism and hysteria' the Prophet controlled and to take advantage of its results.[7]

When it became clear that a number of English-speaking Protestant clerks were assisting Harris in evangelising and teaching the elements of Christianity, the Fathers took the line that the Prophet was an impostor and a tool of 'Protestantism', and Father Gorju's prejudiced account was largely accepted as the Catholic view thereafter. Gorju claimed that Harris hypnotised and terrified the people into believing that he could kill or injure them or even turn them into animals. Even so, Gorju could find no fault with his moral teachings, save to denigrate their significance by saying that, since polygamy was not forbidden ('didn't the Pontiff himself give the example with his *disciples* dressed in white?'), the terrified people did not find it difficult to leave their fetishes 'to embrace this new religion, so uncomplicated in its dogmas and so benign in its precepts'.

Harris's assistants were described as following the same policy of in-

5. Dakar, Report of Chef de Poste, Bongouanou, Nov. 1914
6. Abid. X-46-25, Report of Chef de Poste, Dabou, Nov. 1914
7. J. Gorju, 'Un Prophète à la Côte-d'Ivoire', p. 109

timidation and fraud as their master. They forced the people to build chapels and made them believe the dead could be brought back to life by prayers and hymns. 'Resurrection, if one may express it thus, became the vogue': not that it ever succeeded, but belief in its probability was supported by tales of other villages where it had happened. So the prophets were honoured everywhere, but they,

> far from imitating the prudent and polite reserve of their Forerunner, soon openly showed their hatred of Catholicism, whose ministers they loaded with false slanderous charges, as well as their hatred of the very name 'French'. They openly declared that these hard and demanding masters would soon be chased from the Colony. One of them launched a rumour at the very gates of Bingerville by announcing that a lion from Liberia, where he had already devoured the Catholic Missionaries, was entering Ivory Coast in order to eat all the Fathers and all the French.[8]

This agitator was reported to Father Gorju, and was soon too busy breaking stones for road building to make up any more tales. Father Gorju took the story seriously enough to think that it might refer to the 'Boche tiger' which was present in Liberia in the form of German residents and emissaries. They were said to have told one of the Fathers there, at the time hostilities commenced, that they would make all the trouble possible for the French.

At about this time, from the Cercle d'Assinie, where for a decade ill feeling had increased between the administration and the Agnis, came accounts of a very serious situation, enhanced by the departure of most of the Europeans on the outbreak of war which was regarded as the beginning of a complete and permanent French withdrawal.

THE CERCLE D'ASSINIE

The most easterly district of the Ivory Coast, consisting chiefly of the Agni kingdom of Sanwi, received the Harris faith in a manner peculiar to itself. The repercussions were more alarming to the authorities and, in the end, less rewarding to the church than among the lagoon peoples, and for the same reason.

The chief coastal town in this area was Assinie, founded in the eighteenth century, and a centre for French missionaries and French armed forces. The Agnis had reached the area in about 1820, having been pushed westward by the Ashantis, and the caravan routes to the north led from the coast through the Agni kingdom of Sanwi, with its capital at Krinjabo. For a long time the kings of Krinjabo had allowed no European installa-

8. *Ibid.*, p. 115

tions in their territory, though by a treaty of 1843–44 the kingdom was under the protection of France. After some French traders settled at Assinie, cloth, powder and arms, alcohol and tobacco—the staples of the West Coast trade everywhere—were carried inland. Gradually European influences penetrated the kingdom of Sanwi; Aboisso, not far from the royal capital, was settled by European traders from about 1900, and the traditional agriculture of the region suffered as the people strove to profit from the commercial demand for rubber and mahogany. After 1900 the cutting and shipping of mahogany grew quickly; the 10,000 metric tons shipped from Assinie in 1900 became, after 1910, more than 20,000 tons annually. This growing trade brought new interests and ideas to Sanwi, and groups of strangers, including Fanti Christians and even Muslims from the north, came to live among the Agnis. Coffee was also being grown by 1900 on European plantations and wild rubber was gathered in the forest.

Until 1903 the king at Krinjabo maintained his sovereignty throughout the region save at Assinie itself, and justice was administered by him and his agents. But in 1903, when King G'Ban Konassi died, the French began to administer the kingdom directly, ignoring tradition and the protective relationship they were legally obligated to observe. From the contemptuous way in which the French asserted their authority came the troubles which affected relations between the administration and the kingdom, not only to the end of the French regime but even after the Ivory Coast had gained its independence.

Christianity came with the Catholic missionaries, who started work at Assinie in 1897 and later moved inland. Assinie was essentially a foreign excrescence and offered no opening for the conversion of Sanwi. When in 1900 the missionary Father Bonhomme went to old King Akassimadou at Krinjabo, he was categorically refused permission to establish a mission station in his country. The Fathers had to store their new prefabricated house, brought from Europe, at Assinie, but a few months later the old king died and King G'Ban Konassi then permitted them to build at Aby, on a high hill overlooking the immense lagoon. Pupils came to them for instruction and the Mission seemed a success until all the inhabitants of the village moved away, as was their periodic practice. In January 1904 the Catholic missionaries came to Aboisso and in 1905 built a fine mission house with bricks from their brickyard at Mooussou.

In 1913 economic problems aggravated the political ones. The market for wild rubber collapsed and with it the chief source of money for the inhabitants of the area; the Agnis ceased also to dominate the chief commercial routes to the savannah when the building of the Abidjan–Bouaké railway opened a better route. Yet the taxes imposed by the French administration were demanded as before, and both the Agnis and the local groups of Apollonians were discontented and envious of their kinsmen in the Gold Coast.

It was at this time that Harris hastened along the shore, virtually unnoticed, through 'Big Assinie' and on to 'Half Assinie' in the Gold Coast. Hearing of him, throngs of Agnis and Apollonians crossed over the Tendo Lagoon or the River Tano to witness his power. They followed him to Axim and those who would not come so far met him when he passed a second time through Assinie.

During September 1914, according to the Chef de Poste at Aboisso, although the natives of Sanwi would talk to *him* only under duress, the return of Harris from the Gold Coast had drawn them in crowds to Assinie to be converted and instructed. He was annoyed, but he dismissed the incident as an illustration of the natives' incomprehensible system of values. The newly appointed Administrateur, M. Bru, suggested that while Harris was of no danger at the moment, yet in future he might be. On the other hand, Harris might be of great utility to the administration.[9] Bru found reasons to be dissatisfied with the atmosphere in the Cercle d'Assinie, quite apart from the Harris movement. Neither the natives nor the Sudanese and Senegalese living among them seemed sympathetic to France in her moment of peril and did not respond, as those in other places did, when subscriptions were opened for the war victims.

During October the adherents of the Wesleyan Methodist and Roman Catholic churches were filled with an extraordinary zeal; they were assiduous in evangelising those whom Harris had baptised, and acted in a spirit of rivalry. Each group planted catechists to teach and persuade the truth of their particular doctrines in as many villages as they could. The Chef de Poste had to warn certain villages in the Krinjabo region when some disorders led by rival catechists took place.

During the month the Catholic missionary, Father Bonhomme, travelled through the Cercle, including the Krinjabo area, and his counsels reinforced the warning of the administration in settling the unrest. It was of him or of a colleague that Father Gorju wrote:

> One of our missionaries who was touring in a series of villages where the mere announcements of these events [the marvels associated with Harris] magnified by distance, had caused agitation, did he not also nearly become a prophet despite himself? . . . At the news of his approach the entire population came to meet him, in festive dress, to the sounds of chants and music. He would be led in great pomp to a big hut, newly built. After a new very loud and frenzied series of chants a

9. Abid. X-27-14, Report of Chef de Poste, Aboisso, Sept. 1914, and comments of Administrateur.

deathly hush indicated to him that it was time to begin to preach. All were hanging on his words, but it was not always prudent to warn them against the Prophet Harris; did not one of the assistants affirm to the Father publicly, during a meeting, that he had seen, with his own eyes, at Assinie, the new Messiah take the moon in his teeth!! . . . Some women, in hysterical convulsions caused by the exultation of the moment, would be taken to him and he would pronounce over them a simulated exorcism; these unhappy creatures immediately fell into a cataleptic sleep. Next there was the *auto da fé* of the fetishes burned in a heap in a public spot. At last the good missionary was able to regain his lodging at Aboisso safe and sound. While still under the impression of this uncommon experience he confided to me, one day, that if, unfortunately, the methods of true evangelisation were not other than this, he was confident of being able, by going with a great deal of self-possession and not a little charlatanism, to convert in a few months all the Ivory Coast!![10]

Whoever this priest was, his experience indicates how difficult it must have been for any practising Christian, including the clerks, to refuse to assist people in burning their fetishes and learning the rudiments of Christianity.

Such a degree of religious excitement, combined with the emergency of the European war, gave the administration reason enough for keeping a close watch on developments. By the end of October the situation in the Cercle d'Assinie was becoming unexpectedly complicated. The conflicting groups were interested not only in different forms of Christianity but also in nationalism, which expressed itself in the guise of religion. On the surface it was not black nationalism versus white, but showed itself in the guise of colonial rivalry, English versus French. The converts who chose to become Wesleyans thereby seemed to feel that they had voted themselves English, while the Catholics were to be French. The Administrateur actually warned the preachers that he could admit of no such distinction and that he knew 'in this country none but French subjects.' He reported:

This religious agitation is nowhere but on the surface; it would be a serious misunderstanding of the Agnis to believe them capable of making grave trouble for themselves for the sake of religions to which they are and will be for a long time uncommitted.

I do not believe they see anything more in these discussions than a new chance to waste their time in palavers.[11]

10. Gorju, 'Un Prophète à la Côte d'Ivoire', p. 113
11. Abid. X-27-14, Report of Chef de Poste, Aboisso, Oct. 1914, remarks of Administrateur Bru

Despite his doubts, Bru was impressed by the widespread conversions and destruction of fetishes throughout the inland region, including Sanwi. The Protestants attained that respectability formerly accorded only to the Catholic Fathers when the Methodist Missionary, from Grand Bassam, H. G. Martin (an Englishman) travelled through the district, and perhaps this made Bru think more kindly of the religious upheaval. He still had a great deal of contempt for the reasons behind it. It was largely, he suggested, due to the desire of people to be in fashion, so that the depth and duration of its good effects would not be great; yet, 'I will not risk being precise but on the moral side the natives of Sanwi have very much to learn and acquire; that is why I think we should observe with sympathy the efforts of the Christian missionaries'. It had occurred to him too, as to many others, that with Turkey allied to Germany in Europe, there would be spiritual pressures on the Muslim inhabitants of the French Empire to defend the cause of their religious leader, the Sultan. So he concluded that the Christian missionaries 'could also serve us in the political point of view if (but I do not think that in this region we have anything of the sort to fear), the Muslims, obedient to external instigations, become restless'.

During December religious excitement in the Cercle d'Assinie rose to an even greater pitch and the Administrateur ceased to extract any comfort from it. It was inland, in the Agni country, rather than along the coast with its mixed population, that the greatest alarm was felt. From Assinie, in fact, there was nothing special to report, according to the Chef de Poste, save that the natives were going to bed later because they spent every evening in the church or 'temple' learning to sing hymns. Their singing showed a regular improvement, but so far as honest labour was concerned, they were as uninterested as ever. The Chef de Poste thought that while the Prophet had taught them to rest on Sundays he had forgotten to tell them, or they themselves had managed to forget, that they should work the other six days. 'He has not said more to them than that they should listen to the Whiteman who also desires only their well-being.'

All the villages along the lagoon had built special huts for their religious meetings, and there they gathered in the evenings, filling the days between, as was their wont, with their interminable palavers. Although they had enthusiastically accepted the principles of Christianity, they had not learned the virtues or dignity of labour.[12] Yet this much good was anticipated from their conversion: the high rate of mortality which resulted from the red-wood test and other 'intrigues of fetishism' would be diminished.

12. All the evidence suggests that in most areas where Harris's influence was felt, people did learn to labour and to improve their sanitary arrangements. The Assinie and Agboville regions were thus exceptions.

The Chef de Poste at Assinie, unlike the Administrateur, was not impressed by the results of the visit of the Protestant missionary to the area; Martin had failed to call on him and this may have coloured his feelings. He felt the visit had only stirred up trouble between Protestant and Catholic, calmed only by his warning to both factions, and especially to the English-speaking Protestants, that at the least dissension he would close down all houses of worship.

From Aboisso, in the heart of the Sanwi Kingdom, the situation looked much more dangerous than it did on the coast. The Protestants were, extremely active; nearly every village had been visited by Fanti or Apollonian pastors 'of meagre education and unscrupulous conscience', known in many cases to have an unsavoury past.

These propagators of the faith, left to themselves without supervision and guidance, are at times guilty, through an excess of zeal, of mischievous digressions. The natives have generally admitted that the Catholic religion was that of the French, and that Protestantism was special to the English (French Protestant pastors being very rare in these parts). From that to proclaim that those who would be Protestant should become English is only a step. This step has been taken.

More than this, a rumour is abroad in the country according to which, after the war, France will cede Sanwi and perhaps all the Ivory Coast to England in exchange for another territory, and that those who do not show themselves a little devoted to the English will be severely punished in a few months. The authors and the purveyors of these tidings are still unknown; but it is nearly evident that the Protestant party is not without knowledge of these things. . . .

As a result, the practice of this religion in the region ought to be strictly watched and we ought to demand of the coloured apostles standards of morality and honesty which the majority of them are far from possessing. We could thus check the tendentious rumours and the false ideas which could in the future, from a simple struggle between religious sects, albeit with much in common, give birth to a conflict of nationalities between subjects of one and the same race and nation.[13]

When Bru forwarded the December reports of his subordinates to the Governor, he was so concerned with the situation that he analysed it in depth to discover where French policy had gone wrong in the region. There was no doubting the seriousness of affairs in Sanwi, he thought; the passage of Harris which had led to an upsurge in Wesleyan activity had brought a crisis because it offered the people, for the first time, a

13. Abid. X-27-14, Report of Chef de Poste, Aboisso, Dec. 1914

choice between two religions, and by extension, between two nationalities, French and English. Bru credited the government 'of the neighbouring colony' with not favouring this movement, and even ignoring it, yet he advised that no Protestant churches be permitted in any of the villages, thus preventing the preachers who were English-orientated from winning over the people by their words. He said:

These missionaries should provide themselves with a special authorisation for each religious edifice they desire to open. They should present their native evangelists to us. They should not be authorised to preach in public places and before gatherings save when we are satisfied as to their morals.

On those at present active he said:

The Liberian Harris has chosen his lieutenants exclusively among the foreign Fantis, Apollonians, ex-clerks, ex-shopkeepers, who are far from presenting us with any desirable guarantees.[14]

Bru did not find it strange that the Agnis of Sanwi had lost confidence in the French and looked towards the neighbouring colony of the English. The French, he thought, had always regarded the natives as liars and idlers, meriting neither attention nor study, because in spirit and culture they were so dissimilar to themselves. They had been allowed to become the prey of agents of commerce and business, and of the literate Fantis and Apollonians of the Gold Coast. 'We have not aided them nor defended them against the timber exploiters, miners and others, and after that we are ourselves astonished at not having any influence or prestige among them.' As Chef de Poste at Assinie six years earlier, he had known a happier state of affairs, and on his return to the area in 1914 he had seen signs of regression, not of progress. Villages had become depopulated, family groups had broken up, and no one wanted to take on responsibility as chief of a village or even of a household. There was an obvious mistrust of and an aversion to the authorities. The French had done nothing constructive to mould the indigenous population, and so the initiative for change had passed to the tax-gatherers, exploiters, and the 'self-styled pastors or Bible-carriers' from the Gold Coast. Particular harm had been done to the French 'image' by those colonials who engaged labourers and then refused to pay them. Bru warned the Governor that if serious precautions were not taken, then in a relatively short period of time the French would have only a ruined and depopulated country and, moreover, 'the evil influence we have fostered here will gain ground and infect neighbouring cercles'.

14. Abid. X-27-14, Report of Chef de Poste, Assinie, Dec. 1914, remarks of Administrateur Bru

THE EXPULSION OF HARRIS

Despite the alarming turn of events in the eastern district of the colony, most of the Cercle des Lagunes seemed by December to have settled down peacefully enough to practise its new faith and to please the officials by a show of industriousness. The Chef de Poste at Dabou had escorted the head of the Agricultural Service around his district visiting promising plantations, among them that of Victor Nivri at Addah. Everywhere were the new churches, and there was no sign left of any other worship than Harris's. In the vicinity of Abidjan there was not the same spirit, due to the fact that Protestants, natives of British colonies, had been warned by the administration to stay away from villages where they took part in ' a religion which was not theirs'.[15] No doubt it was feared that *Protestant* and *English* would be equated there, as in Sanwi. Without the help of the clerks, there was no one to instruct in the new faith, and it lagged.

Only around Agboville was there trouble. Besides the usual evasions of duty and the flight of people to the bush when they knew the Chef de Poste was approaching, the four villages of the Azaguie group were hostile. They refused to clear their roads, to prepare palm nuts, to collect kola nuts, or even to honour the contracts into which they had entered voluntarily with the timber merchants. The leaders of this resistance were to be found at Aoua (a village some 40 kilometres from Abidjan) which was also a centre for the new religion. Chief Adou, who had been hiding in the forest and directing the party hostile to the French since the suppression of 1910, attracted support through the new faith and he spread the rumour through the region that two government officers had already died for persecuting the new Saviour and that others would share the same fate. He was only one of a number of die-hard old warriors still fighting the French underhandedly.

In the Cercle de Lahou a wave of religious enthusiasm had been raised during September by the preaching of Samuel Reffell, the disciple of Harris, but there was nothing political about it. It did lead to numerous baptisms. During October there was unrest in the upper part of the Cercle, especially in the Lakota-Zikiso area. It was not identified by the Administrateur as part of the religious movement; Apollonians, Fantis, and Sierra Leoneans were credited with causing it by spreading rumours that the Germans had invaded French territory and that the French were on the verge of being defeated.[16] At about the same time, the Didas of Lozoua gave proof of their ill-will by refusing to provide porters to carry supplies inland to Lakota. Finally, on 10 December the Prophet Harris himself arrived again at Lahou.

15. Abid. X-46-25, Report of Chef de Poste, Abidjan Rural, Dec. 1914
16. Abid. X-39-4, Report of Administrateur, Cercle de Lahou, 3rd quarter 1914

Administrateur Corbière at Lahou was not keen on having Harris in his district, and was pleased to hear from him that God was recalling him to the Gold Coast. After one full day at Lahou, Harris started eastward but at the edge of the Cercle (presumably at Kraffy again) he halted, and crowds went to him to be baptised.[17] The Administrateur was aware of this but as he thought Harris was not exercising any harmful influences he did nothing about it. Three churches had been tolerated in Lahou for some months: one for the Avikams, who had been warned against allowing false disciples of Harris to mislead them and take their money, one for a group of Apollonians and Fantis who had been in the town a long time and wished to worship under a Catholic Father, and a Protestant Church attended by several hundred people from the Gold Coast and Sierra Leone.

Angoulvant, despite his personal good-will towards Harris, was obliged to consider whether, at a time when the country was upset over the war, the economic crisis, and the withdrawal of administrative personnel, it might not be safer for the religious movement to be dampened down. The reaction to the new faith on the part of such groups as the Ebriés, Adjoukrous, and Alladians showed no special anti-government tendencies, but the strange expectations being reported from the eastern and northern parts of the Cercle des Lagunes were alarming.

At Bingerville it was decided that Harris must be sent home and the new religion must be stamped out of existence. On 16 December a confidential memorandum went out to all administrateurs:

From information coming to me from different sources it appears that the moral-improving activity of the 'prophet' William Wade Harris is interpreted in a different fashion by the natives and is hampered in a rather unfortunate way mainly by his imitators, improvised pastors recruited from among clerks severed, often for delicate reasons, from their counters.

So it is that one Administrateur has told me about the rumour circulating in his *cercle* that Harris was going to succeed in obtaining before long a reduction in the rate of tax and even the suppression of the *capitation*.

In the impossible situation in which the much-reduced personnel of the *cercles* now find themselves, the doings of these more or less religious personages (we do not really know who they are or where they come from, or what are their real intentions) cannot be watched closely enough, therefore you will, without being abrupt, rid your area of these people. You will invite the pretended 'sons of God' who have been

---

17. Abid. X-39-4, Report of Administrateur, Cercle de Lahou, 4th quarter 1914

roaming to the villages recently to return to their own country where they will be able to spread the good word easily. The Prophet Harris in particular will find in Liberia, his own country, a sufficiently vast field for activity.

This measure is necessary at a moment when the events in Europe demand more than ever the maintenance of tranquillity among the people of the Colony, and for that you must prevent the birth and circulation of all false news which might upset the people.[18]

The details of the expulsion of Harris are not clear. Since he was at Kraffy when the decision to expel him was made, he was evidently arrested there and taken to Lahou. Presumably it was at this time that, as Harris later told Benoit, Administrateur Corbière

asked me why I always continue to preach. I said to him, 'I am a prophet like Elijah—to destroy the fetishes.' But then they acted like pagans, they mocked me and said, 'The Bible is no good.' I said to them, 'I stand up to witness for Jesus Christ.' But they burst into laughter and said, 'You are only a Kruman to row and carry hammock, that is all. You cannot teach us.' But I read to them from the Bible, Acts 5:39, 'If this work be of men, it will come to naught, but if it be of God you cannot overthrow it,' then they began to abuse me, 'Dastard, idiot of a Kruman,' and they led me away to prison.[19]

Harris and the three women were carried to Dabou and then to Abidjan. They were stripped and beaten, their calabashes and the cross broken, and their money and clothes stolen. Mrs Hannah Johnson and other friends living at Bassam sent money and clothes, bribing the guards to deliver them.[20] Six months later, Father Gorju described the same incident unsympathetically thus:

Harris himself, having made an ill-timed reappearance at Abidjan, was apprehended without respect, stripped of his sacred staff, had his beautiful robe replaced by a common worn loincloth and finally was expelled from the colony. The time had passed when this crafty individual, profiting by the similarity of names recognised, as an incarnation of his protector the Archangel Gabriel, the person of the Governor of the Colony, who was astonished at this celestial origin which he had never suspected.[21]

18. Dakar, Confidential Memorandum from the Lieutenant-Governor of the Ivory Coast to Administrateurs of the Cercles, 16 Dec. 1914
19. Benoit's Report
20. Benoit's Report (account from Mrs. Hannah Johnson)
21. Gorju, 'Un Prophète', xiv. p. 116. The Governor, of course, was Gabriel Angoulvant.

Local tradition is misleading on this imprisonment at Abidjan, putting it prior to the time Harris preached at Bingerville under the Governor's benign eye. According to them, he came out of the locked prison every morning by miraculous means and the brutal guard, Kouacou, who had broken his cross, was found burnt as if by a thunderbolt.[22] Another account says Kouacou died when Harris clashed his calabash while sitting on the threshold of the prison,[23] but this is told in ignorance of the smashing of those calabashes. It testifies at least to the awe felt for the power of the calabashes that this story was told, and that in it Harris was set free by the Governor.

In actual fact, he was taken to Bassam and held there until a ship came by which he could be sent home. Crowds of people came to see him depart, and tradition says that he was searched by the authorities to see whether he had taken a great deal of money from his converts. The point of this story is to prove that he had taken nothing, but had the seven shillings and sixpence with which he claimed to have started from home. A quite different version tells of a much larger sum, the correct amount for the passage of himself and the two women[24] to Cape Palmas, put in his baggage miraculously.[25] Father Gorju said the women were discovered to have seven thousand francs in their possession, but he did not term it a miracle.[26]

A quite different account of Harris's departure, putting the administration in a much better light, has been given wide currency through Methodist missionary accounts. Captain Marty, in his account published in 1922, stated that when the request to return home was put to him, 'Harris, always dignified, started back, his pilgrim's staff in his hand, towards Cape Palmas'.[27] A few years later, when F. D. Walker of the Methodist Missionary Society was in the Ivory Coast collecting facts about Harris, he was given a full and moving description of this dignified exit. The officer, M. Paoli, had gone to Port-Bouët in April or May 1915, on hearing by rumour that Harris was holding a service on the shore. Here he preached

22. Oral evidence of Mathieu Adobi and Abraham Nandjui
23. Oral evidence of the Preacher, Methodist Church, Songon M'Brathé, Aug. 1963
24. There were only two women to go with him, since Grace Thannie from Apollonia returned home at this point. One of the two Liberian women was unsophisticated and from the bush, and since she later bore Harris a son (Benoit's Report), may be counted as his wife. The other was Mrs Helen Valentine, a cultured person, widow probably of the Rev. M. P. K. Valentine, priest of the Protestant Episcopal Church (see p. 14). Mrs Valentine had seen signs in the sky and in visions which hed her to accompany Harris, according to information gleaned by Benoit. Her injuries received in prison in Abidjan were so serious that she died soon after returning home.
25. Daniel Aka Coblan.
26. Gorju, 'Un Prophète', p. 116
27. Marty, *Etudes sur l'Islam en Côte d'Ivoire*, p. 18

and baptised while Paoli observed him, and when the service was over and the officer told him he had come to escort him to the frontier, he went with him meekly.[28]

Possibly this was a return visit by Harris, but administrative records make no mention of any attempted return before the end of 1915, and then he was stopped on the frontier.[29] The same records give no details of the manner of his expulsion, but the order was given, as shown, in December 1914, and in the same month began the full scale suppression of the movement; it seems incredible that Harris could have been wandering about freely during a further four months.

Moreover, the French Vice-Consul in Monrovia, M. Baret, who had been asked in December to inquire into Harris's antecedents, reported in February that Harris had been expelled from the Ivory Coast and was in Cape Palmas in January (1915).[30] It seems most probable, in the light of this evidence, that Government agents later wished to appear more benign in their treatment of Harris than they were in reality.

The expulsion of Harris did not halt the progress of the religious and social changes he had set in train. In the Gold Coast the Methodists and Roman Catholics freely competed to win over his converts, and new religious communities appeared as well. In the Ivory Coast, on the other hand, the expectations of the converts were so much at variance with the policies of the government, and the Christian missions were so weak, that for some years the official attitude was that the new religion should be totally suppressed, and since the missionaries by their activities might keep it alive, every discouragement was put in their way.

From the beginning of 1915, as official records show, churches were being ruthlessly destroyed, especially in the Cercle des Lagunes, where force could be more easily deployed. The officials were heartened when some of the elders among the Abbeys in the Agboville region assisted in the arrest of one of the new 'Sons of God' agitating there. In the Dabou region some converted villages were refusing to pay the tax. Numerous Abbeys were coming down from Agboville to be baptised by Djibi, a native of the village of Gomou. Because of the widespread commitment to the Harris faith shown in the Dabou area, the Administrateur decided to be cautious in disturbing the churches, lest too much public unrest be provoked.

During February 1915 the Cercle, especially in the Agboville region, was overawed by the presence of the 5th Senegalese Tirailleurs, and with

28. Walker, *The Story of the Ivory Coast*, p. 19
29. Abid. X-21-441, Political Report for Ivory Coast, 1915
30. Dakar, Report of French Vice-Consul, Monrovia, to Minister of Foreign Affairs, Paris, 19 Feb. 1915.

their support the Chefs de Poste of Dabou, Agboville, Adzopé, and Alepé toured their areas to destroy churches, relocate villages on the main roads, and to give the *coup de grâce* to 'the new religion, which was no more than a means of opposing our authority'.[31] The Chef de Poste at Dabou made a point of searching among the Abidji villages for any Abbeys who had come to the 'false prophets' there; he found some of them at Yakessé, where Djibi (he believed) was accepting their money in return for baptising them. Djibi fled into the bush as the officer approached; the latter burned down the church on Sunday evening (7 February) and Djibi was caught and carried to Dabou to be tried. The same officer found *campments* around Yassap and Orbaff where groups of Abbeys had been staying while awaiting baptism, and these he destroyed. He lectured the villagers wherever he went on the folly of supporting the 'prophets' with their money, and though he did not forbid them to hold services, he ordered them not to pay those leading such services.[32] This officer felt that the new religion had less hold on the Abidjis than among the Adjoukrous and Alladians, and in some villages (such as Ababou and Bécédi) the chiefs had closed the churches and forbidden services as soon as they heard of the arrest of Harris. They declared that they wanted no palavers with the government.

When the same Chef de Poste toured the Alladian Coast in March, collecting taxes from the scattered population and burning the illegal hamlets, he found two or even three pastors in every village and felt compelled to suppress them, because they had assumed a commanding place in village affairs. On the mainland he found an excuse to destroy the church in the large Adjoukrou centre of Débrimou, on the complaint of one of the elders, Katakre, that it was causing dissension among the inhabitants.

If the officials had wished, they might have been able to control the new religion by placing it firmly in the hands of the Catholic missionaries, depleted though the number of Fathers was by the obligation of mobilisation. The official view, however, continued to be opposed to the work of the Catholic Church. This was made very clear in a short exchange between the Administrateur of the Cercle des Lagunes and the Lieutenant-Governor in June, 1915. On 20 June, the Administrateur forwarded the request of the two villages, Anoumabo and Abobo-Doumé (both facing Abidjan across the lagoon and today in its suburbs) for permission to build a church in durable materials to be handed over to the missionaries for Catholic worship. This was a test case, and was so regarded by the

31. Abid. X-46-26, Report of Chef de Poste, Agboville, Feb. 1915, and comments by Administrateur
32. Abid X-46-26, Report of Chef de Poste, Dabou, Feb. 1915

officials. It was decided to discourage the trend unequivocally; the Troisième Bureau which advised on religious matters commented: 'The natives would do better to employ their time and money in planting cocoa instead of buying, probably from Mooussou,[33] expensive bricks to construct a church as a free gift to the Mission. The Mission would doubly profit from that.'[34] The Lieutenant-Governor's official advice was: 'Tell the villagers they can easily cross over to Abidjan on Sundays to attend church there—it would be a chance for them to have an excellent Sunday stroll.'[35]

The religious suppression thus undertaken was ostensibly in the interests of the war effort. Applied against both Catholic and Methodist evangelists, it forced people to look for spiritual authority outside organised Christianity and in direct defiance of the government. Ultimately, the government was to regret this, but in the summer of 1915 it was complacently assured of the complete eclipse of the new faith. In actual fact it was being practised in secret, and where the churches were destroyed, people simply met for their services somewhere else. In October 1915 there were rumours from the Adzopé area that disciples of Harris were active and that churches were being rebuilt, while at Dabou in November 'a Sierra Leonean' who tried to revive the Harris religion was put in prison. In the region of Jacqueville, as the Chef de Poste discovered when he went over in December to distribute school prizes, people were actively trying to revive their churches. The Chef de Poste promised to watch them and arrest them when necessary.

In the Cercle d'Assinie events were following a different course. Religious suppression, coupled with political unrest, and the proximity of a refuge with kindred peoples in the Gold Coast, led to serious migrations. When the news of the arrest of Harris reached the Agnis of Sanwi, and dashed their expectations that he would win better conditions for them, there was a sizable exodus over the frontier. This took place in January 1915, as the taxes became due, but it had other causes, including a serious quarrel between the leading Protestants and the 'king', Kadia Kassi. An inquiry by the Chef de Poste showed that economically the Canton of Krinjabo was in a desperate economic situation. Kadia Kassi was accused of not distributing money he had received in payment of timber rights and was extremely unpopular. Although people were deep in debt, they refused to produce palm oil and the few cocoa-farmers refused to sell their produce on the grounds that prices were too low.[36]

33. At Mooussou, near Bassam, the Catholic Fathers ran a flourishing brickyard.
34. Abid. X-46-26, Correspondence: 3e Bureau to Lieutenant-Governor, 26 June 1915
35. Abid. X-46-36, Correspondence: Lieutenant-Governor to Administrateur, Cercle des Lagunes, 29 June 1915
36. The commercial slump was a consequence of the war. Tauxier, pp. 190–2

Aministrateur Bru, despite his analysis in December 1914 of the manner in which the French had betrayed the best interests of the Agnis, was perhaps not the man to inspire confidence in French intentions. He no doubt revealed by his attitude his suspicion of some secret understanding between the British officials across the frontier and the people of his Cercle. He agreed with the Chef de Poste at Aboisso who reported that 'a current of secret propaganda emanates from the neighbouring colony', and was himself convinced that the District Commissioner at Half Assinie was offering large sums of money to emigrés from Krinjabo if they would make plantations in his district.[37]

It seems certain that the new religion was used by the Agnis of Sanwi as a bond solidifying their opposition to the French administration and all its works: its attempts to make them exploit their resources for the benefit of commerce, its taxing and recruiting activities which were a violation of the original treaties of protection, and its contempt for native institutions. Many of those who went over the border settled there permanently. In 1916 there was a new exodus when it was incautiously let slip that sixty men were to be conscripted from the Cercle. Aboisso was deserted at once, and when Bru called all the chiefs together there, they met beforehand with the king of Krinjabo and instead of accepting quotas, as Bru expected, they decided not to cooperate at all. On 26 December 1916 they too went into Gold Coast with their wives, families, and supporters, leaving the Cercle more than half empty of its inhabitants.

Methodist leaders in Britain believed that the Agnis had emigrated because of their religious convictions and believed, as they publicly said at their May meetings in 1915, that the return of a large number of exiles to Krinjabo earlier that year had resulted from the promise of the Administrateur that the church would be rebuilt at government expense. In fact, no such condition was agreed to, nor does religious freedom appear to have been a serious issue in subsequent efforts to bring back later groups of exiles. When in 1917 the chiefs, rebuffed in their attempt to put their country under British protection, submitted the conditions upon which they would return, these were in effect a demand that the laws of the Ivory Coast should not apply to Sanwi, for they wanted no taxes, no forced labour, no recruitment, and no alienation of the forest lands. But they did not request any religious concessions. In June 1918 the Agni emigrés agreed to return under a complete amnesty, and although there was still a period of tension, French power was ultimately confirmed and a king and elders more friendly to the administration were soon put in control.

It is impossible to avoid the conclusion that the Agnis accepted the

---

37. Abid. X-27-14, Report of Chef de Poste, Aboisso, Feb. 1915

baptism of Harris as a vehicle for embarrassing and alarming the French, and as a source of internal strength and unity. They were not prepared to use it for the changing and modernising of their society; they made no effort to work the six days before resting the seventh, nor does it appear that public and private hygiene, or public morals, improved; education was not sought, and society as a whole was not motivated positively. Rather, the attempt was made to turn the clock back. The rumours that Great Britain would annex the region (in 1917 the Agnis invited the British in the Gold Coast to do so) and that Harris was having the head tax lowered, or even abolished, were an indication that Agni sentiment was looking to the political past, not to a spiritually refurbished present. The very rivalry between Protestant and Catholic suggests a political contest, not a spiritual one. Even though the Catholic converts had opted to be 'French', hoping perhaps to wring some advantage from the administration, they too fled to the Gold Coast in large numbers when no such advantage appeared.

The subsequent religious history of this region is of little interest, indicating the failure of Harris to arouse a lasting spiritual response among the Sanwi peoples.

CHAPTER NINE

Evangelists, Prophets and Missionaries

D URING THE YEARS of World War I the Prophet Harris continued to wander and preach, but his converts of the Ivory Coast and the Gold Coast did not see him again. While he was wandering westward they were exposed to a variety of missionaries, bogus prophets and independent evangelists of varying degrees of sincerity. Furthermore, those in the Ivory Coast were subject to an almost continuous suppression by the government for more than ten years. Nonetheless, out of the two hundred thousand or more people who were moved to burn their fetishes, tens of thousands remained faithful and waited for the messengers Harris had promised.

In the Gold Coast, the government put no restriction on religious activity, so the Catholic and Methodist missionaries were able to work freely among the Harris converts. They had what would normally be considered a great success, but they did not succeed in bringing in all the converts. The Church of England, which was a minor element on the religious scene of the colony and had no missionary working in the area Harris visited, benefited unexpectedly from the zeal of the 'Bishop of Sanwi', John Swatson. Swatson evidently had an affection for the episcopal tradition, for it was to the 'English Church Mission' (of the Society for the Propagation of the Gospel) that he pointed his converts.

Swatson was born at Beyin, followed his commercial career in Nigeria, retired to the Gold Coast, and in 1912 and 1913 was appointed Methodist agent in Aboisso. In 1914 he became a fanatical follower of Harris, who consecrated him as his 'bishop'[1] and apostle for Sanwi and the frontier area of the Ivory Coast and the Gold Coast. Swatson returned to Aboisso but then continued along the caravan route north and wandered into

---

1. Marty, *Etudes sur l'Islam*, p. 17. Mr Paul Jenkins, University of Ghana, has delved deeply into Swatson's relations with the traditional religion and with the Anglican Church, and will be publishing his findings in the future.

British territory. During the next few years he preached to the Sefwis, Aowins and Denkyeras and his efforts brought him into conflict with chiefs and district commissioners who viewed the destruction of the private and public fetishes as tending to dissolve all moral sanctions. The congregations Swatson established required more direction than he could provide, while the catechists he recruited soon became dissatisfied with their financial prospects. The English Church Mission had already heard of the unorganised congregations of the 'Christ Church Mission— Beyin', which were apparently set up by Swatson on an Anglican rather than a Methodist pattern. Soon after Easter 1916 Swatson visited Archdeacon G. W. Morrison at Kumasi and offered him the fruit of his labours. Morrison toured the area and was warmly received by the converts during a period of three weeks, and in June Swatson and his workers were officially appointed as Anglican agents. Swatson soon settled at his old home, Beyin, where he helped translate the Prayer Book and hymns into Nzima, and drew many Methodists and Catholics into his large congregation. In the area he evangelised the Anglicans built wisely on his foundations. His baptism was accepted as valid and in due course Bishop O'Rorke confirmed the converts. Polygamists were accepted as adherents and were not denied full Christian burial. The work lived, and the cocoa farms made in 1916 as an endowment for the churches are still supporting many of them.[2]

In Nzimaland itself many Harris converts joined strange new cults in which the traditional religious ideas and practices of the area were blended with the Christian ideas derived from Harris. Although its leaders honoured the Bible, they were illiterate and not able to refer to it directly. The cults which they developed were, in the eyes of the missionaries, a 'bastard type of Christianity . . . infinitely worse than raw heathenism'.[3] The chief figure in this syncretistic faith was Grace Thannie or Tani, who is said to have been a fetish priestess at Kristen Eikwe up to the time Harris arrived. She was baptised by the Prophet at Axim, but showed an unusually stubborn evil spirit. Accounts differ as to the degree of success Harris had with her, but apparently she joined his entourage because he did not feel she was fit to be left on her own. When he returned to the Ivory Coast she went too, clad in a white robe, carrying a calabash and joining the two Liberian women in leading his services.

When Harris was expelled from the Ivory Coast Grace Thannie returned to Nzima. She called herself Madam Harris Grace Thannie and tried in some way to carry on Harris's work. She and her followers, 'prophets' and 'prophetesses', dressed in white, shook beaded calabashes

2. Oral evidence of Canon C. H. Elliott, Cape Coast, Sept. 1963
3. M.M.S.-G.C., Witter to Thompson, 4 June 1923

Grace Thannie II, who claims to be head of the Twelve Apostles Church in **Ghana**. Photographed at Ancobra Mouth, 1964

and sang as well as they could the Kru hymns Harris had introduced. Their aim was the exorcism of evil spirits, which was to them the meaningful part of the Prophet Harris's work. Naturally, they charged clients fees for their services.[4]

Madame Thannie called her church 'The Church of William Waddy Harris, and his Twelve Apostles'. She claimed that it knew no boundaries of race or tribe, but believed 'in God's Mercy and the beneficial influence of *His Holy Word*'. Through 'their unbounded faith in God Almighty', her priests effected miraculous cures and performed wonders. They did not claim, she assured the authorities, to be able to exorcise witches, nor detect witchcraft, nor to practise black magic in any form themselves.[5] It can be assumed that in describing her religion she put a Christian gloss on it which may not have been deserved.

Within a few years of the foundation of the sect, water-carrying began to play an important part in the ritual of exorcism and healing. Presumably the idea developed from Harris's practice of baptism. It formed part of the healing service which soon became the major part of Thannie's work. The sick held pans of water on their heads while the singing of the Kru songs and the clashing of the beaded calabashes set up a rhythm which sooner or later sent them into a trance or state of possession. In this they swayed or even danced feebly, splashing water out of the basin over themselves. When they became quiet again the water remaining was carefully taken off and used as a personal medicine to be applied both internally and externally.

It seems likely that the idea prompting this was that an angel of healing descended during the trance and transformed the water into holy water. Early in the sect's existence there was a belief that the water became salty as it became holy.

Various imitators of Grace Thannie sprang up in Nzimaland and even east of Axim. At some time she joined forces with another convert of the Prophet Harris called John Nachabah (or Nakaba). He made his headquarters at Essuawah, near Tarkwa, and later, when he had built up an organisation, claimed to be 'Founder and General Chairman of the 12 Apostles Mission'.[6] The present widespread 'Church of the Twelve Apostles' regards these two as the 'pioneers' who carried on the work of the 'founder', W. W. Harris.[7] By the church's own admission, these 'pioneers' were illiterate, and it was only through the assistance of more

---

4. Cape Coast, C. 733, Report on Harris Sect by A. Q. Kyiamah, submitted 6 Feb. 1940
5. Cape Coast C. 733, Petition from Madam Harris Grace Thannie of Christen, Axim, 17 Jan. 1940
6. Cape Coast, C. 733, Letter from John Nachabah to Chief Commissioner, Cape Coast, 25 Aug. 1947
7. An official almanac of the Twelve Apostles Church (seen in 1963)

educated leaders, some of them formerly pastors in other churches, that a widespread network of congregations and some sort of centralised church government was built up.

Besides this organisation, many individual prophets and prophetesses evidently rose and flourished for a time. One interesting group was formed at Alluapokeh, not far from the town where the infant Kwame Nkrumah was learning the rudiments of the Catholic faith. It was founded by Cudjoe Monnor, a former Catholic who was able to give 'power' to suppliants, who claimed to cure with holy water and prayer, and who built up a chain of congregations probably second only to the Church of the Twelve Apostles. Known originally as 'Kagyeletpah' or the Healing Power Church, it was renamed, under Cudjoe's son, St Anthony's Healing Power Church.

It is clear from these developments that the Nzima converts did not respond completely to the message of the orthodox and European-centred churches. Many reverted to traditional practices again, and witchcraft, which had seemed for a time to be uprooted, reappeared. This tendency, in an area where the Methodists and Roman Catholics already had a firm footing, could not have been anticipated in 1914, when Harris ordered his converts to join one church or the other. In some cases the religion offered by the churches was not to the taste of the converts; these became followers of the syncretist groups described above. Many others were never really contacted by the churches, and though sometimes they were nominal Christians, they were very ignorant ones.

Among the Methodists certain factors weakened the mobilisation of resources for the task of attracting Harris converts. When, six years later, another Prophet, Sampson Oppong, appeared in Ashanti, the English missionaries there utilised the most modern forms of transport for control and built up a large Methodist community.[8] Not only were there no modern forms of transport available in Nzimaland at the time, there were no English missionaries either. The one African minister in the circuit had only a handful of trained assistants, and the wonder is that he accomplished as much as he did. The deployment of a larger number of both African and European clergy would have borne permanent fruit.

Methodist membership climbed from 961 full members, 1037 on trial, and 4132 catechumens at the end of 1914 to 2387 full members, 1524 on trial, and 3048 catechumens in 1915 and to 3049 full members, 3461 on trial, and 2079 catechumens at the end of 1916, by which time the decline in catechumens suggests that the Church had attracted the majority of potential converts.

8. G. M. Haliburton, 'The Calling of a prophet: Sampson Oppong', *Bulletin of the Society for African Church History*, ii, Dec. 1965, is a recent description of this movement.

The Synod of 1917 replaced Bruce by James B. Graham, who remained at Axim until 1922. During his years the hollowness of much of the Methodist achievement became evident. John Swatson's church at Beyin had drawn away many Methodists from that area, and even where there were no rivals, the shortages of staff and the defections of unworthy agents had harmed the work. On Armstrong's tour of the area in May 1916 he had found that many of the congregations 'on trial' did not understand any of the 'doctrines, duties and privileges of the Christian Religion'.[9]

The Methodist community in the Ivory Coast, which was governed by the Gold Coast Synod, was not able, officially, to do as effective a job with Harris converts as Bruce and his assistants in the Axim Circuit. Yet indirectly, more effectively perhaps for being unofficial, they greatly influenced the converts in the Ivory Coast and laid the basis for a future Methodism amongst them. The Church had begun among the English-speaking Africans at Grand Bassam in 1896, under the leadership of John A. Bonney, a tailor. Later on the work was annexed by the Dixcove Circuit, which put Bonney in charge as lay agent. Land and buildings were donated at Bassam by the Hon. John Mensah Sarbah of the Gold Coast, and one of the buildings became the first church.[10] From about 1909 the work was under the Superintendent Ministers of the Axim Circuit, and it grew to include congregations at Aboisso and Assinie. Few if any of the members were Ivoirians.

The Methodist Synod of 1914 created a new circuit under Bassam with the name 'Ivory Coast Mission', and it was assigned an English missionary, H. G. Martin, and an African assistant minister, J. C. Koomson, who had already been at Bassam as district agent. Martin arrived from England in September 1914, but though he saw the effects of the work of Harris, he apparently did not meet the Prophet or show any curiosity about his methods. He later reported with approval that 'many young men who had come from British districts and had received an elementary Christian training were employed by the people to minister in these churches and give religious instruction'.[11] Following the arrest of Harris and the suppression of his churches, the Government had restricted Martin's movements. In his report to the 1915 Synod he said that 'patience, tact and judgment' were called for, and could only hope that 'someday' permission would be granted for missionary work in the villages.[12]

The centres in which faithful Methodists could be found in 1914,

9. M.M.S.-G.C., Armstrong to Goudie, 26 June 1916
10. M.M.S.-G.C., 'Report on the Ivory Coast' by H. G. Martin, 2 July 1916 (he cites as a source the Rev. J. Reynolds, African minister)
11. M.M.S.-G.C., 'Report on the Ivory Coast' by H. G. Martin 2 July 1916
12. *The Gold Coast Annual, 1915*

according to the subscription lists, were, besides Grand Bassam, Assinie, Aboisso, Abidjan, Bingerville, and Half Jack, while stations planned for the coming year included Mooussou, Bonoua, Krinjabo, Vietri, and Alepé. The adherents at these latter places were certainly native Harris converts.

After returning from the 1915 Synod, Martin was able to gain an interview with the Lieutenant-Governor and, though he was forbidden to station agents in the villages, he was given leave to go himself and preach in those villages where chapels had been built. Reporting this, he was forced to admit that 'those men who have been going about preaching to the people and taking money from them on their own account, have not helped my work; this irregular evangelism has encouraged the Government to adopt repressive measures and to regard Protestant Missionary work . . . with suspicion'.[13]

In March Martin toured the Assinie-Aboisso area and made his peace with the offended Chef de Poste at Aboisso. While promising that Wesleyan preachers would not stir up trouble,[14] he requested permission to station one at Krinjabo. He had to submit his request to the Governor, and as he feared, it was rejected. At the same time both Catholic and Protestant missionary work was prohibited in the whole district except in Aboisso itself. Martin felt the government's fears were groundless and said that the destruction of churches and scattering of catechists, 'Protestant, but not under our control, reflects little credit on French Colonial Administration'.[15]

The 1916 Synod proposed no changes in the Ivory Coast Mission, ignoring, in his absence, Martin's suggestion that Half Assinie become its headquarters and an educational centre. A few months later Martin concluded his Ivory Coast service with a report on the situation and his recommendations. He belived that, despite Government opposition, the Church was making progress. The most urgent necessity was a centre for the education of the children, and this the government would not allow. He recommended that a French-speaking European missionary be sent out to supervise the mission, with a French-speaking African teacher to start an elementary day school. He also urged negotiations with the government in Paris for permission to station evangelists in the villages and towns, as desired by the inhabitants, to build churches there, and to open day schools for the Protestant children.

When Martin's successor, Edmund C. Horler, arrived at Grand

13. M.M.S.-G.C., Martin to Goudie, 3 May 1915
14. Abid. X-27-14, Report of Chef de Poste, Aboisso, Mar. 1915
15. M.M.S.-G.C., 'Report on the Ivory Coast' by H. G. Martin, 2 July 1916

Bassam he was told he could preach and visit only in the town. He secured an interview with the Lieutenant-Governor, who firmly refused to permit him to evangelise, on the grounds that it was the missionaries who were causing political trouble and confusion among the natives.

> No amount of explanation could convince him that natives who were good Christians could not fail to be better citizens. The final result of the interview was that no Missionary would be allowed to visit any of the villages in the Colony and that I must not even visit the stations we have already in existence.[16]

The Governor recapitulated his arguments in a letter. He stressed the damage which preaching at large would do to the war effort by deflecting the minds of the inhabitants from their duty. In the circumstances, Horler had to send away without hope the many village deputations who came to welcome him and request his aid in rebuilding their churches and giving them instruction. Since he was useless at Bassam, the Synod of 1917 decided to use his services in the Gold Coast, and he returned to the Ivory Coast only to report his departure to his flock there.

Horler spent the next three years exploring the region along the Tano River and in the Aowin and Wassaw Districts of the Gold Coast. He found ignorant catechists carrying on Methodist work of a very low order, in which the collection of class dues played the largest part. He found certain native kings hostile to the spread of Christianity; the Omanhene of Enchi was especially difficult, for he said the Christians could not keep goats, as Horler had suggested, because it offended 'the Tanor fetish', while the 'King's fetish' was spoiled if people worked on Tuesdays and Saturdays.[17]

In 1918 Horler took charge of this area, which, as the 'Apollonia Mission', was made an independent circuit. He hoped to establish its headquarters at Enchi, but this was never done. Horler was not able to return after his furlough in 1920, and after several drifting years, the 'Apollonia Mission' was dissolved as a failure.

There are apparently no detailed figures on the Methodist community in this region which might document the pessimistic conclusions of the missionaries. However, the record of full members in the Axim Circuit (including the Apollonia Mission) indicates a curve reaching its apogee in 1921. In 1913, before Harris came, there were 633 full members. In 1915 there were 2387; in 1917, 3405; in 1919, 4138, and in 1921, 4737. This figure rapidly declined to 2959 in 1924, and continued to decline generally

16. Min. G.C.S. 1917
17. M.M.S.-G.C., Horler to Goudie, 19 Apr. 1919

thereafter.[18] By that time, no doubt, the water-carrying cults were making serious inroads into Methodist ranks.

Although we have no detailed accounts of Roman Catholic work during this time, one source states that between 1916 and 1920 Father Fischer baptised about 4000 persons, mostly adults, and that by 1921 forty stations had been opened in Nzima country, with ten more along the River Tano.[19]

18. Wesleyan Methodist Church, *Minutes of Conference*, 1914–25
19. M. J. Bane, *Catholic Pioneers in West Africa*, p. 184

CHAPTER TEN

The Harris Legacy

IN THE IVORY COAST the situation remained basically one of holding to their new faith against attempts by the administration to root it out and turn them into rationalists of the approved kind. They showed their lack of interest by following certain self-styled successors of Harris, such as Do and Yessu[1] who expounded additional and rather inferior doctrines, or by listening attentively to Mark C. Hayford, who hoped to bring them into his 'Baptist Church Mission and Christian Army of the Gold Coast', with its headquarters at Cape Coast. Because of official animosity none of these men had much success, but their appeal made it evident that secularism would not prevail. In 1919 the Protocol of St. Germain regarding freedom of conscience, religion, and missionary rights in Africa was signed among the victorious Powers, and it seemed possible that if the French Roman Catholic missionaries were not encouraged, religious manifestations of a hostile nature to the government might appear. So it was a turn-about when on 11 November 1920 (the anniversary of the Armistice) the Lieutenant-Governor attended a singing of the *Te Deum* in the Cathedral at Grand Bassam.

Subsequently, when the application of the Protocol was laid down by decree in 1922, the threat of English-speaking Protestantism was fended off by declaring that no English or foreign vernaculars were to be used in religious services. The Wesleyan Methodist community, largely of Fanti origin, was in despair. Fortunately, their appeal for help was answered by a young English missionary, W. J. Platt, who was in charge of Methodist work in Togo and Dahomey. He convinced the Governor that the Methodists would adapt to the law, and that Protestant Ivoirians would be as loyal to the administration as Catholic ones.

1. Dakar, 'Au Sujet propagande religieuse dans la région Abidjan-Dabou', Report of Administrateur L. Bourgine, 28 May 1920.

The Methodist Church in Great Britain had lost sight of the Harris community of the Ivory Coast, about which they had never received a full report. It was a great surprise to them when Platt, after touring the colony in 1924, revealed that tens of thousands of converts had been patiently waiting for ten years for the white man with the Bible promised by Harris. Despite financial difficulties the Missionary Society undertook to set up a full-scale effort to take these converts under its wing, and black personnel from Togo and Dahomey, as well as white missionaries from England and France, were sent in. The effort met with a great success, though it was impossible on their limited resources to answer all the appeals from Harris converts for catechists and teachers.

Many of the Harris converts had already become Catholic, while others valued too much the loose ecclesiastical structure which had developed among them to become Methodists. Platt naturally hoped to bring all Harris converts into his fold, and in 1926 became worried by news that Mark Hayford was soliciting funds in Europe to establish his Baptist Mission among them. He decided to send an envoy to Harris, who, it had just been discovered, was still alive, and to get, if possible, his blessing on the Methodist work. So the Rev. Pierre Benoit, accompanied by one of Harris's interpreters, Victor Tano, took passage on the German steamer *Irmgard* for Cape Palmas. They landed on 23 September and soon found Harris.

In the years since he had left the Ivory Coast, Harris had continued to evangelise, but although he had often been able to arouse a wholehearted response to his preaching, he had never again stimulated a mass movement of the Ivory Coast–Apollonia kind.

A very interesting and sympathetic account of him was recorded soon after he left the Ivory Coast by Father Peter Harrington, S.M.A. Father Harrington, an Irishman, met Harris at Grand Cess in May 1916, while doing pioneer work on a new mission station. He had read Gorju's fulminations against Harris in *L'Echo* and was initially inclined to attack him on the lines of Gorju's criticism.

In the conversation as reported, Harris laid great stress on the miraculous aspects of his calling. His costume had been given to him by Gabriel after he had miraculously escaped from the prison at Cape Palmas, leaving his old clothes behind. Gabriel had then accompanied him as a travelling mentor on his journeys. The gift of tongues had enabled him to preach in French—but he might 'exercise this great gift only for the preaching of the Word, and it comes and goes as the Spirit wills'.[2]

When Harrington questioned him on the reported threats of his Ivory

2. Harrington, 'An Interview with the "Black Prophet"', *The African Missionary*, 1917

Coast disciples, that a lion would come to devour the Catholic fathers and other whites, and about the rumours that the disciples were German sympathisers and Harris himself a German agent, the Prophet grew furious and said; 'What could I know about the Germans? What are they to me? I am a Prophet of the new dispensation of Christ. How can men write such things about a Prophet of God? Can black men sit down with Germans and talk friendly as we talk now?'

Harris then explained that he was one of twelve prophets commissioned by God to work in the modern world. Four of these were assigned to Africa, Harris having West Africa as his charge. He was (at the time of this interview) on his way north to Sierra Leone to meet with his colleague of the north. When the great blood-letting was finished in Europe, they would meet there to dictate to the rulers of the earth the conditions in which the rule of Christ on earth, the millennium, would begin.

When the missionary accused Harris of altering the doctrine of Christ, for example by permitting polygamy, the Prophet was troubled. 'Man, don't you see?' he said. 'The Prophets can dispense—they cannot change. . . . Like the prophets in the Old Law, we may grant certain dispensations until the reign of Christ is fully established on earth.'

Father Harrington was unable to make up his mind whether Harris was a clever impostor or a fanatical maniac, but he did hope that his visit would boost the prospects of the Catholic Mission at Grand Cess, especially in counteracting the ill-will caused when a 'fetish grove' had been cut down by the missionaries, with the chief's permission, as a site for their mission station. The missionaries were invited by the Prophet to attend the great meeting he had called, because 'our church was the mother of churches and the public prayer would not be complete without our presence'. Accordingly, the missionaries attended and found the chiefs and even the most enraged fetishmen present in all their finery.

The Prophet spoke to the meeting in both Kru and English. His terrible voice could be heard to the extremities of the town, and as he thundered he varied his movements, standing still for a time then running and jumping, always gesticulating. His message was that the people must destroy their fetish objects and join the Christian church. He was full of praise for the Catholic Church, but to Harrington it seemed he knew little of it save that it was the 'old church, the big church, and the mother of churches'. When he called on all to kneel and pray with him, the old chiefs and fetishmen knelt too.

A few days later Harris passed on towards Monrovia and Sierra Leone, ignoring the war which was raging around him.[3]

Father Harrington concluded his account by saying:

3. In 1916 another serious rebellion had broken out among the Krus.

At all events the fetish-doctors of Grand Cess gave us no trouble whatsoever after the visit and denunciations of the Prophet, and whatever the good man may imagine or believe as to his mission and the 'new dispensation of Christ', I am happy to assure him that his abhorrence of and propaganda against Fetishism was most helpful to our infant mission station at Grand Cess, and I think also to the Old Dispensation of Christ as promulgated by its time-honoured prophets, the twelve Apostles.

By July 1917 Harris had arrived in Freetown and began preaching to the Kru community there. According to a local newspaper:

He preached of death and destruction to the world because of sin. He carried a Staff with a Cross at the top end and a 'Shake-Shake' (a calabash with beads strung loosely over it), this he said was a 'Bell' calling people to assemble to hear him and a 'harp' to captivate the multitude. He also denounced the Priest of every church. He led people into fits of ecstasy with songs and many a time the vast throng would fall unconscious.[4]

Here he soon had the reputation as a healer, and a paralysed woman was cured when he held his Bible on her head and prayed over her.[5] He baptised those who had confessed their sins and thrown away their fetish objects, and as he went through the streets of Krutown a multitude followed him.

His reputation suffered a shock when he disappeared suddenly, taking with him two well-educated young ladies who had taken part in his services dressed as prophetesses. The Kru community believed he had used hypnotism to bind the girls to him. There was therefore no continuing congregation of Harris converts, but many of the converts joined one or another of the churches of Freetown.[6]

Harris meanwhile wandered back to Liberia, where he spent the remainder of his life, since he was never permitted, though he tried, to enter the Ivory Coast again. He was seen again in 1919, preaching in the streets of Monrovia, and concentrating his efforts on Krutown, along the harbour. Evidently he failed to have his usual success, for standing on the edge of the high ground on which Monrovia is built, he hurled maledictions on the sinful lives of the people in the shabby town below. He threatened it with destruction by fire. Less than a month later a serious

---

4. *The Weekly News,* Freetown, 4 Aug. 1917
5. Letter from Bishop E. J. T. Harris, Freetown, 18 Aug. 1964
6. Letter from S. H. Robin-Coker of Freetown, 19 July 1965

fire destroyed a large part of their town and the Krus, who had been so indifferent to his preaching, attributed it to his power.[7]

Harris continued to preach unnoticed until 1925, when he deeply offended the Methodist missionaries at Nana Kru. The missionary in charge, the Rev. W. B. Williams, had been on friendly terms with Harris. Williams's ideas of the active role played by the Holy Spirit in combating Satan were not unlike those of Harris. For example, he wrote thus of the descent of the Holy Spirit on the girls at the Mission School:

> School was in session, but books were pushed aside. Indeed it was impossible to attend to lessons. As soon as the opening chapel service began, the power of the Spirit would fall. Our students would be prostrate on the ground, praying and praising. Farming was imperative with close to a hundred mouths to feed, but the ground remained untilled. The revival had right of way, while a hundred souls were born of God.[8]

One is not surprised to learn that Harris often stayed with Williams at the Mission House.[9] However, a change seemed to come over Harris, and Williams published the following account of it:

> God's Avenging Sword silencing the lips of a great enemy to the Lord's work among the Krus came with supernatural force in 1925 on Nana Kru Mission. Up to a year ago, in his wanderings up and down the land, the old Prophet Wade Harris, of Ivory Coast fame, was a frequent visitor at this station. Sometimes he stayed for days and at times for weeks, sometimes accompanied by his two wives, sometimes alone. . . . I have known him personally for more than twenty years. I visited him when he was in prison at Cape Palmas for treason, and prayed with him in his cell. That was before he proclaimed himself a 'prophet'. And from personal knowledge of the man these many years I can testify that he has done our work great harm by living himself in polygamy, preaching polygamy, and baptising polygamists.
>
> When the epidemic of flu was raging he visited this Mission, staying in a house in Bethany Town, the Christian settlement on the Mission compound where our married students live with their families. There had been five deaths that day. I had conducted the five funerals and urged the people to turn from their sins. I felt worn out, but God so stirred my spirit that I went down to pray and reason with the old

7. Oral evidence of the Rev. J. D. Kwee Baker, Monrovia, 2 July 1963. Presumably they believed Harris had called down fire from heaven.
8. W. B. Williams and M. W. Williams, *Adventures with the Krus in West Africa*, p. 79
9. Letter from the Rev. W. B. Williams, St Petersburg, Florida, 16 Oct. 1965

prophet. For he had been proclaiming all along the coast, in the towns where our Methodist churches were established: 'Jesus Christ had twelve disciples and they were men. I shall have fourteen disciples, and they will be women. This polygamy talk is white man's mouth. Black man no need to trouble his head about it.'

With burning heart, I began to talk and plead with the old man. I could not pray with him, for he would never unite with us in prayer. At a prayer service he would sit down, open his Bible, get up, walk around the room, go out of doors till we were through. So I pleaded with him and gave him all that was laid upon my heart. Before I was through, Wade Harris fell on the ground, caught my foot, and almost screamed: 'For God's sake, Williams, leave me! Leave me! Don't talk to me any more!' I said, 'Wade, I will never open my mouth to you again on this subject. I have given you what God told me to give. It is now between you and your God.'

He went away. At intervals he renewed his visits here. In 1925, after one of these visits in Bethany Town, he went on to Newer Point where we had a church and hundreds of children in our Sunday School. He called the town together and said to the people: 'You can have all the women you want. I have just come from Williams' Mission and talked to them there and all their men begin to take other women, and I have broken up the Mission. What Williams says is just white man's talk; don't hear him.'

Then he passed on, spreading his lie wherever he went.

It was unfortunately true that just about that time two of our younger men in that town had fallen into sin with women and had been dismissed from the Mission.

Our people were troubled and reported what the prophet was saying about the Mission and how he was baptising all kinds of men who had more than one wife. They asked, 'Teacher, you no fit to stop him?' We answered, 'Wait. God reigns.'

There came a day when the prophet turned back to Cape Palmas, and in due course the high road led him past Nana Kru Mission. With averted head he pursued his way, down the road to the beach and across the Mission lagoon. And when *just outside Bethany Town, where he had gone out to spread that wicked lie, God struck him to the ground, paralysed and dumb*! Our own preachers went to his assistance and half carried him into the town and into one of their houses, where we nursed him back to partial health. We wrote to his people in Cape Palmas, and we secured a boat to carry him the hundred miles to his home, but he rose up very early one morning and walked off, dragging his paralysed leg and able only to utter a word here and there that was intelligible. . . .

Since that day, he has visited here, and has partly regained the use of his limbs and tongue, but he tells us: 'I can't preach any more.'[10]

When Benoit met Harris in September 1926 he was evidently so far recovered that he gave no impression of being incapacitated. He was delighted to meet Benoit and Tano, and they had long talks. Precious photographs were taken of Harris holding his feathered cross, painted in red and blue, and wearing on his neck the new Huguenot cross which Benoit had brought for the purpose. This would prove to all doubters in the Ivory Coast that Harris was a Methodist. Benoit told the old man about W. J. Platt and suggested he might like to recommend him to the Ivoirians. He agreed that he would. Similarly, when Tano told him the Methodists advised their people to read the Bible and to follow the ten commandments, he agreed that this was good. Even the phrase 'Jesus Christ our only Saviour' caught his fancy, and he incorporated it along with the other phrases in the three letters he dictated to Benoit at the latter's request.[11] The first letter was a general communication to all his Ivory Coast followers, telling them to become Methodists and not Roman Catholics, to accept Platt as his successor, to shun fetishes, to read the Bible and observe the ten commandments and the word of Jesus Christ. The second letter was to the chief of Grand Lahou, telling him and his people to become Methodists and to wear the Huguenot cross, and the third brief note to the Harris converts at Fresco was to the same effect.

Benoit returned in triumph with these letters, but they did not have the influence in the Lahou area that he hoped. Many *Harristes* did become Methodists, but more would not; the stumbling block was the missionaries' insistence on monogamy.

Platt was delighted with the general letter and with the photographs identifying Harris as a Protestant and (since one showed Benoit and Harris shaking hands) a friend of the white missionaries. He sent them to London to have 500 copies made of each so as to be able to pass them out to the village churches.[12] This had the desired effect: in most areas the independent churches became Methodist.[13] Platt also intended that the Missionary Society in London should feature the contact with the Prophet in the daily press and in the *The Foreign Field*, as missionary propaganda. However, Thompson, the West African secretary, was sure that the facts would disappoint and disillusion many people. 'They have never realised

10. W. B. Williams, *God's Avenging Sword*..., a promotional pamphlet printed Sinoe-Kroo Coast District, 25 Dec. 1928, pp. 5–6
11. Benoit's Report
12. M.M.S.-F.W.A., Platt to Thompson, 26 Nov. 1926
13. Holas, 'Bref aperçu sur les principaux cultes syncrétiques de la Basse Côte d'Ivoire', p. 57

how exceedingly crude and elementary was the religion of this man and how great is the work now to be accomplished by the Christian Church.'[14]

Although Mark Hayford did put in an appearance in Bassam and Dabou in May and June 1928,[15] he found the Methodists firmly in control of the congregations with whom he had treated in 1919 and the government unfriendly. If Hayford had been able to speak for an organisation with resources during his previous visits, and if he could have guaranteed to inculcate obedience to authority and love for France in the Harris converts, and had recruited European colleagues, the administration might have accepted him. In that case, those who later became Methodists and Catholics, and those who remained aloof as Harristes or who drifted back towards fetishism, might have formed a native African Church of some importance under his direction.

A greater threat to the Methodist work in its most promising area, Adjoukrou country, emerged when an Alladian, Bodjo Aké, appeared and began to work as a prophet, claiming that he was Harris's son. He baptised in pig's blood and preached polygamy.[16] He criticised practices of the Methodist missionaries severely, saying that they were only woodcutters and that their object in coming to the country was to rob people of their money. He composed a defamatory hymn which he sang everywhere, naming every missionary and holding up to particular ridicule de Billy, the French missionary in charge at Dabou.[17] The missionaries brought a case against Aké and he was sentenced to five days in prison and 300 francs fine, the Mission receiving 1 franc in damages. The prison sentence was not enforced and Aké went on as before.

It was evident that the support for Aké came from the vested interests which the missionaries were undermining. Those who did not like Methodist discipline united with certain village chiefs and the old men who were annoyed at seeing their dignities usurped by young catechists from Togo and Dahomey to oppose the missionaries. The returned soldiers, the literates and semi-literates, who had always led opinion and controlled the villages, resented the setting up of schools, the translation of the Scriptures into local languages, and the breaking of the monopoly of knowledge. The administration was to a certain extent sympathetic, and the Roman Catholic elements were agreeable to opposing Protestantism.

In January 1930 W. J. Platt announced his resignation as leader of the Methodist Mission. He returned to London to take up another post,[4] not only because his health had deteriorated, but also because he felt the

14. M.M.S.-F.W.A., Thompson to Platt, 3 Jan. 1927
15. M.M.S.-F.W.A., Platt to Thompson, 21 May 1928 and 20 June 1929
16. *Ibid.,* 6 Dec. 1926
17. M.M.S.-F.W.A., Fletcher to Thompson, 5 June 1927

The healing garden of the Twelve Apostles Church, Kormantine, near Salt Pond, Ghana; headquarters of Prophet George. Photographed 1963

Prophets and prophetesses of the Twelve Apostles Church, Ghana, 1963

Ivory Coast Jubilee, 1964 (celebrating the fiftieth anniversary of the Prophet Harris's arrival in the Ivory Coast). The President of the Ivory Coast leaves the Methodist Church, Abidjan, after the induction of the first African Chairman. (l. to r.) the Rev. W. J. Platt (first Chairman), the Rev. S. Nandjui (new Chairman), President Houphouët-Boigné and (in background) the Rev. E. de Billy

Village church elders, Ivory Coast Jubilee, 1964

W.M.M.S. was not making adequate provision for the District nor giving him, as director, sufficient support.[18] It was a great shock to the clergy who had served under him and, as the Rev. E. K. A. Gaba wrote, if the French no longer suspected the Wesleyan Mission of being 'a secret agency of England in the French colonies to entice the Natives away to British rule', it was due to Platt's prudence.[19]

The departure of Platt brought to an end the period of missionary pioneering among the Harris converts.

Today those who joined the Methodists have their own autonomous Eglise Protestante Methodiste in the Ivory Coast, and the colony to which the missionaries came is now an independent country in which Ivoirian Methodists are respected and active citizens. Blyden and Harris could have asked for no better realisation of their dreams.

18. M.M.S.-F.W.A., Thompson to H.L. Bishop, 17 June 1930
19. M.M.S.-F.W.A., Gaba to Thompson, 12 Feb. 1930

CHAPTER ELEVEN

The Last Days of Harris

WHEN PIERRE BENOIT had visited Harris in 1926 the old man had been excited to hear of the fame he still enjoyed in the Ivory Coast and he expressed the wish to return there with the missionary. Benoit firmly discouraged him. He would have presented the Methodists with many problems had he appeared in the flesh, whereas the letters he signed and the photographs for which he posed could only help them.

It has been suggested that these letters, which so strongly commended the Methodist missionaries to his converts, did not express Harris's real thoughts. Certainly those who wish to believe that Harris was trying to found a new 'African' church would find it unthinkable that he would have signed these letters. They were, after all, directly intended to undermine the existence of such a church, whether it grew out of his original teaching or from the activities of Mark Hayford. One can only say that there is no evidence that he thought, when carrying out his original preaching, that an independent church was possible or desirable. He had always told his converts to join churches where these were established, and where there were none, he told them that missionaries would one day come.

Despite this, he would never have thought of writing to his Ivory Coast converts to command them to become Methodists had Pierre Benoit not come to him. When Benoit did come, it was natural for him to do as he asked. Fragile and perhaps a bit senile, his fire burning lower, he was flattered by the fact that a European missionary had travelled hundreds of miles to find him and do him honour. Benoit had told him of the esteem in which he was held by the great Methodist Church in Britain. He had told him of the thousands of Ivoirians who held his memory dear and still observed his commands. Benoit solicited his help

The Prophet Harris poses with the Rev. Pierre Benoit at Cape Palmas, 1926

and good-will for the Methodists. The cumulative effect of these attentions to one starved for a little appreciation of his great work and divine calling was to win his acquiescence to the proposals put before him. He could not have said to Benoit the words some of his Ivory Coast converts wished: 'I preach that we have no need of the White Christ and His white missionaries. I preach a faith for Africans only, based on the struggle against evil which we were fighting long before you white men came. I preach the power of God and His angels to drive out devils, to punish sorcerers and evil-doers, and to reward the righteous. I preach that one day the black man will be his own master again, and that the white man will perish in everlasting agony.'

No, this was not the sort of stuff to tell Benoit, and so the missionary went away with the commendation he had sought. But another embassy from the Ivory Coast appeared in March 1929, and this time a declaration on the lines sketched above would have been well received. The envoys were two men, Solomon Dagri and John (or Jonas) Ahui, son of Akadja Nanghui, the chief of the small village of Petit Bassam. They stayed with Harris for some weeks, and it appears that the old man was happy to give his blessing to them and to let them carry on their work independently of the Methodists. At any rate, their account was that they came asking Harris to teach them how to check the ravages of death among those who remained faithful to the Prophet's teaching. Looking over them, he spoke to the younger, Ahui (then about thirty-four), and said, 'You shall carry on my work'. He bestowed a Bible and other sacred articles on him, thus inaugurating a church which, since World War II, has become a strong rival to Catholicism and Protestantism in the Ivory Coast[1] and has absorbed almost all the congregations which had carried on the Harris tradition independently. It is known as *l'Eglise Harriste*, the Harris Church.

Ahui claims that he was ordained by Harris as his successor on 23 March 1929, and that in the several weeks he remained with him, Harris laid down rules for the church. These were sensible and constructive: schools should be opened for the instruction of the children, prayers were to be in the vernacular, preachers were not to covet the wives of their neighbours, nor to drink alcohol (or be drunk in public), nor to provoke fights. Apparently nothing was said about polygamy, but it was conceded that if a man's wife were ill or absent he might take a 'friend', but when his wife was with him again, he had to tell her what had happened and what gifts he had given to the friend.[2]

1. Holas, *Le Séparatisme religieux*, p. 270
2. Oral evidence of Prophet Jonas Ahui and his son Paul, including typewritten notes by the latter, Petit Bassam, Aug. 1963

On his return to Petit Bassam, Ahui attracted followers and gradually acquired influence over the nearby villages where people were dissatisfied with their churches.[3] He and his people believed that Benoit had concealed a large part of what Harris had told him, including a forecast of the end of French rule in the Ivory Coast.[4] They believed also that Harris had intended to found a Black Church and that this church had been strangled by missionary intervention.

The instructions Harris gave were grouped into ten commandments which were circulated among the independent congregations, and in the course of time a catechism in which their ideas of God, the Church, and Ahui were expounded.

One official difference between the Harris Church and the Methodist was the emphasis the former put on spiritual healing. Even today they stress that the penalty for sin is sickness. Its cure entails a confession before the pastor and elders of the congregation, who thereupon pray for the sinner. This was, of course, standard practice in many of the village churches before Platt came and is still, unofficially, often the practice in Methodist churches.

Ahui was the last visitor entertained by Harris, who was dead within a few months of the former's return home. When the news of his death reached London (11 October 1929) the *Daily Telegraph* devoted several columns to him. *L'Echo* in February 1930 gave him its final notice, suppressing most of the ill-natured things said in the past, commenting only:

> He demanded nothing, accepted nothing. He refused to attach himself to any sect but recommended his converts to join any Christian Church. He was a born orator, speaking in an abrupt and harsh language and gifted with a singular penetration; his achievement was considerable.

> Without approving the theories and teachings of this free-lance Evangelist, a singularly cautious free-lance, the Catholic missionaries have admitted without difficulty certain advantages for the Catholic religion from the preaching of this improvised prophet. An old missionary who had had the occasion of seeing him close said of him:
> 'He made no exception for persons and he pursued with his orations governors, chiefs, princes and kings. Although he made no distinction between sects and religions yet he openly proclaimed that the Catholic church is the true church and that it would have been agreeable to him

---

3. In 1949–50 Jonas Ahui visited the independent Harris Churches of the Cercle de Lahou and succeeded in winning over a majority of them. The rest, who remained loyal to their leader, Ledjou N'Drin Gaston, call themselves *L'Eglise Harriste Biblique* and in 1963 claimed 32 congregations.
4. Jonas Ahui

to see all the people bound there. He had asked us to go establish a mission in his own country, promising to support us. I regret to say—but it is my inner conviction—that the Christians come out of the Harris movement are not those most firm in the faith, contrary to what has been said in papers and reviews.'

The Protestant missionaries attribute to the preaching of Harris an important movement of conversion in the Ivory Coast. As to the Catholic missionaries they are satisfied to see in his case a typical example of the religious mentality of the West African Negro.
Pierre Benoit pronounced the Methodist judgment when he wrote:

Harris is, in part, a figure from the Old Testament, but there is more than that in him. There is even more in him than in John the Baptist, who was not the last page of the Old Testament but the first page of the New. Harris well represents what a black Christian prophet could be. He symbolises for the native of the bush all that revelation can be for him. He carries the law and grace to the heart of societies so little evolved as those of the Africans.[5]

What can we finally say about Harris and his movement? To begin with, we can describe Harris as a Christian, dedicated from the time of his conversion when he became a Methodist lay preacher to winning his people from the power of the evil spirits which, it would seem, he believed existed, but he also believed they could be overcome with God's help. Although he became an Episcopal catechist it does not appear to have represented a change in belief, rather, as he told Benoit, he did it 'to make money'. Evidently permanent service in the Episcopal Mission was more secure and better rewarded than brick-laying, while his zest for preaching could still find its outlet.

His idea about the right way to preach to his own people must have developed during all the years since he had come into contact with Christtian teaching, and it may have been hearing or reading the speeches of E. W. Blyden which stimulated certain tendencies. As we saw in Chapter I, he announced his intention of shedding European-type clothing at the same time as he was evidently planning to start a Grebo revolt, but it does not appear that he had any intention of being any less a Christian preacher. As we have seen, he did abandon European clothing when he came out of prison, but whereas we can infer that in 1909 he intended to combine a religious and political role, whereby the Grebos might be independent of the Liberians and where a synthesis between Christian ethics and African culture might flourish, the events of 1910 had put an end to his political dreams, and when he emerged from prison it was as a Prophet in the

5. M.M.S.-F.W.A., Benoit to Walker, 5 May 1929

spiritual sense only. In the eyes of his family and neighbours he was mad when he came out of prison and put on his white robe and turban, but as we have seen his behaviour in 1908 and at the time he raised the Union Jack was certainly unconventional and unpredictable; in a way there seems to be no sharp break between what he was and what he became. After a long journey he had reached his goal.

The prophet who emerged from prison seemed to have been purged of all his old bitterness against the Liberians, and took no interest in politics or the plums of government favour. He had entered a world in which these things were as insubstantial as shadows. If he could bring his own people and their neighbours, bring all West Africans, to the worship of God alone, then the millennium would approach so quickly (the time when, he told Father Harrington, he would be giving orders to kings) that the little troubles of Liberians and Krus would be dissolved in the universal kingdom of God on Earth. In the meantime, as he said, he would grant dispensations to Africans for their peculiar institutions (in particular polygamy) until the will of God was made clear on his arrival. It may be that Harris felt that on this and other matters Jesus would confirm his view and not those of the white missionaries.

One might have expected him to be disillusioned with his understanding of God's plan when war ended and he was not called to Europe, but no doubt he supplied himself with reasons to explain it. He had behind him his amazing Gold Coast–Ivory Coast experience, which fortified his faith in his prophetic calling so that no subsequent rebuff or disappointment could shake it. To the end of his life he retained a strong sense of his mission, and though in his last years he was not the preacher he had been, he still played his assigned role with all the dramatic intensity he could muster.

Can we now make a judgment on Harris? So far as his personality is concerned, we have seen that he was a man of volatile temperament and of wholehearted dedication to action. Long before he came out of prison as a prophet he occasionally ran into danger and risked the anger of authority, characteristics which were, if anything, intensified when he began his prophetic preaching.

The reality of his call from God is not something we can judge. To Harris it was a true call and he believed he was guided in all his travels by the Archangel Gabriel. Under this guidance his concern was altogether with spiritual, not secular, matters, although change on the spiritual front led of course to a variety of other changes.

We have seen that what he did in the Ivory Coast in particular in modifying or even revolutionising the religious ideas, the concepts forming the foundation of the whole social order, brought about a change in the whole social structure. In the particular conditions of the Ivory Coast situation Harris, by undermining the traditional beliefs in the gods and spirits of every sort, threw many assumptions into a state of flux. What he preached was consistent with that he had been taught by the Methodist and Episcopal missionaries, but given a more precise local application, more sympathetic to the beliefs and needs of the people. This aspect of his teaching may have been due entirely to his own mature reflections based on his experiences among his own people, or it may have developed under the (conjectural) influence of E. W. Blyden, or even a bit under the stimulating tongue of Casely Hayford during the thrilling weeks at Axim.

We seem to see a double point of view exposed in his commands. When he condemned all spirits, regardless of type, and the whole system of taboo, and when he condemned every type of worship or act of respect towards the spirits, such as the pouring of libations, he was true to the missionary code. But when he used his influence to modify old customs and institutions instead of condemning them, thus strengthening them instead of trying to substitute for them the culture of the white man, as missionaries were prone to do, then he showed himself to be of the school of Blyden and Casely Hayford.

The position Harris took when true to his own better judgment seems to modern thought to have been much more enlightened and akin to progressive missionary ideas than the nineteenth-century missionary view which he reflected when he condemned traditional gods and spirits (along with more recent arrivals) as creatures of the Devil. The worst fault the missionaries could find in the Prophet Harris was that he defended polygamy, which they equated with 'immorality'. Their case is not as easily accepted as they and the Western society which sent them out supposed and representatives of the latter still suppose. Missionary literature through the years shows a blindness to the practical social good of polygamy and a determination to regard the licence it gave a man to have permissible sexual relations with a number of women as equivalent to adultery. Without arguing at length, it is fair to say that the element of 'immorality' has been vastly overemphasised in the missionary point of view, and that there are other points of view which put the case for polygamy very strongly. The Prophet Harris was not a renegade and traitor to Christ because he saw polygamy with African and not European eyes.

In what ways other than in his teaching was Harris more acceptable than white missionaries? His very act of disowning European culture completely by robing himself in a gown and turban set his style clearly. He was seen to be an African, not a European and not a Europeanised African. He was stranger even than a white man, but less alien. Another favourable factor was his passion for his mission. He was inspired and fanatical; he was a prophet twenty-four hours a day. He had not chosen to be a prophet, it seemed, but had been chosen, unlike missionaries who are men wedded to a routine of daily life in which inspiration may be kept in check.

Whatever else Harris may have been, he was both sincere and, usually, wise, and his efforts followed a recognisable and sane pattern. The fact that he lived a life so different from most men stamps him as being *peculiar* by ordinary standards, but all saints and prophets are peculiar when judged against the norm. What makes Harris notable and admirable is that he succeeded in stamping his personality and commands so widely and deeply that ten years after he left them vast numbers still remained loyal to him.

As a charismatic figure fit to win the confidence of people, Harris stands far above the general run of missionaries and compares well with other African prophets of the same generation. It was in fact a time of prophetic movements, his nearest contemporaries being Lotin Samé in the Cameroons, Garrick Braid in the New Calabar region of Nigeria, Simon Kimbangu in the Congo, and Sampson Oppong and John Swatson in the Gold Coast (Ghana). The first three seem to have preached to people already strongly influenced by Christianity and in many cases church members. Like Harris, Samé and Braid favoured an Africanising of Christian discipline, and their acceptance of polygamy was one example of this. On the other hand, Simon Kimbangu in the Congo evidently forbade polygamy, along with such innate cultural expressions as drumming and dancing. Like Harris, all three fought against witchcraft and sorcery.

Oppong and Swatson, both (probably) inspired by Harris, preached like him to a population little affected by Christianity, and like him persuaded a large number of people to abandon traditional beliefs. Their converts were soon integrated into the Methodist Church and the Church of England respectively, and it seems clear that neither had the presence and the charismatic influence of Harris, nor the authority to modify tradition rather than destroy it.

The individuality of Harris when compared with these others seems to lie in his success in bringing a whole people to him without raising up antagonistic and disruptive forces. The other preachers mentioned all encountered varying amounts of antagonism, not only from European officialdom but from chiefs, clergy and groups of people. Yet Harris for the most part was respected by all until the officials felt themselves pushed by events.

With respect to charisma, Harris and Simon Kimbangu seem equally impressive, though some writers give the impression that the latter adopted many traditional techniques of sorcerers in order to fight witchcraft and perform his miracles. There is certainly little evidence of this in Harris, who seems to have adopted Christian symbols and sacred literature to his needs.

Out of Kimbangu's movement religious and political movements were born, and the development which took place veered into channels not followed by the majority of the Harris converts, for the latter made the movement the vehicle for an adjustment to the colonial situation and of co-operation among themselves so as to benefit from the new conditions it brought.

This brings us to the other factor involved in the degree and kind of success of a prophet, the situation of the people to whom he preaches. There was in the Ivory Coast when Harris arrived a sharp-edged confrontation of cultures, particularly acute since Angoulvant had assumed office and narrowed down the field of independent activity left to the native population. This was the situation in which old standards, practices and beliefs seemed to have lost their ability to guarantee peace of mind and stability. Increasingly the Ivoirians were becoming part of a money economy, exchanging plantation crops for European luxuries which were soon classed as necessities. With this material change came a malaise in society; the ready adoption of new cults, such as that of Mando, indicates the widespread feeling of insecurity. The frequent poisoning of vigorous young men, whether by the priests of Mando, by evil fetish practitioners, or in tests for witchcraft, gives the impression that a death wish lay on the people.

The great value of Harris was that he changed this despondent situation into one of hope and purpose, where people applied themselves to solving their problems from a new set of premises. It cannot be said that he elicited the same response everywhere; the nature of anyone's reaction to him depended on the circumstances. Not all responses were really constructive. The Agnis of Sanwi used the new faith only as a means of defying the French. The Didas found in it a justification for refusing to pay taxes and for resisting French claims to suzerainty over their country. In similar fashion, the inland Abbeys, Attiés, and Agnis thought the new religion would relieve them of the colonial burden. The Gold Coast converts form no easy pattern; some of them probably had these same expectations, that life would become simple again and the European would cease to disturb it. Others saw with the people of the coastal regions of the Cercle de Bassam, Cercle de Lahou, and especially with most of the Ebriès, Adjoukrous, Abidjis, and Alladians of the Cercle des Lagunes, that the clock could not be turned back, that the European presence and the modern commerce which accompanied it had come to stay, and that the new faith would help them to cope with it. These were the people who ultimately, in both colonies, either joined the two missionary-dominated churches or remained independent, but definitely repudiated the traditional religion of the past.

Of course Harris brought no golden answer to the problems of 1914 which could satisfy people's needs forever. He had inaugurated a very important stage of religious and social development. He had done away with past burdens, but there could be no final solution to ever-changing problems. Once the first stage had been accepted, smaller adjustments had to take place, and circumstances or taste brought new solutions to new anxieties.

Harris's real legacy today is the adjustment so many of his converts and their descendants have been able to make in a changing world. It is the many men and women in Ivory Coast and Ghana who through his commands were given an education and who constitute a strong body of intelligent and alert citizens in those countries. There are no figures available of the actual numbers involved, but the several Protestant churches of the Ivory Coast and the Catholic Church there contain active clerical and lay leadership which has played its part in the realisation and sustaining of Ivory Coast independence. Similarly in Ghana many outstanding people owe to Harris their education and their ability to make a useful contribution to their country.

His legacy is also to be found in the various churches which regard him as their founder and which try, through the power of his God, to bring health and happiness to their members. Today these churches, the Eglise Harriste and independent groups in the Ivory Coast, the Church of the Twelve Apostles and the Harris Church in Ghana, speak to people for whom the orthodox churches have no appeal and, syncretistic or only partially Christian though they may be, continue to preach of the love of God and his interest in his children's welfare, and his continued readiness to send spiritual help to them through their pastors and healers.

Select Bibliography

W HEN I BEGAN research into the life of the Prophet Harris it was with
a sense that there was an urgency about it, because of the fact that
by 1962 there was a fast dwindling band of those who had seen him in the
flesh and who could throw fresh light on his personality and career. Even
in the year or two before I could travel down the Coast and meet the elders
in their villages, valuable sources of information were lost as old people
passed away or lapsed into senility. Nonetheless, I did have valuable meetings with eye-witnesses of events which were to them of fundamental
importance in their subsequent lives. The contributions of these old men
were noted in many footnotes through my pages; I only hope the reader
will not feel that the necessity of presenting them as part of an academic
exercise has washed out the excitement and awe revealed in my notes
taken on the spot.

I was concerned also to find more official evidence about the activities
of Harris. Very little of the published material made any bow in the direction of official files. My starting-point for getting a picture of the accepted
view of Harris was to read W. J. Platt's *An African Prophet* (London, 1934).
This account forms a watershed so far as information on Harris up to the
present is concerned, since it drew on all published sources up to 1934,
and has been the basis for most of what has been published since. The
present volume is intended to be a leap beyond Platt's account, and while
it is based on some new material, it supplements rather than supersedes the
older book, and throws a different light because of a different point of
view.

Platt's account, which is the view of a committed and scholarly missionary who publicised the Harris Movement when it was virtually unknown, was based not only on his own experience but on several other
sources. There was the report (in manuscript) of the Rev. Pierre Benoit

who visited Harris in 1926, and a pamphlet *Le Prophète Harris* issued in 1924 by M. Jean Bianquis of the Paris Evangelical Missionary Society. He had been able to refer to Gaston Joseph's *La Côte d'Ivoire, le pays, les habitants* (Paris, 1917) and Paul Marty's *Etudes sur l'Islam en Côte d'Ivoire* (Paris, 1922), as well as other sources. Other sources available to Platt included J. E. Casely Hayford's *William Waddy Harris, the West African Reformer: The Man and his Message* (London, 1915), C. W. Armstrong's *The Winning of West Africa* (London, 1920), Georgina A. Gollock's *Sons of Africa* (London, 1928), F. Deaville Walker's *The Day of Harvest* (London, 1925) and *The Story of the Ivory Coast* (London, 1926), Arthur E. Southon's *More King's Servants* (London, 1929) and L. Tauxier's *Religion, moeurs et coutumes des Agnis de la Côte d'Ivoire* (Paris, 1932). Important articles on Harris, which Platt may not have seen, included J. Gorju, 'Un prophète à la Côte d'Ivoire', *L'Echo des Missions Africaines de Lyon*, XIV, 4, Sept.–Oct. 1915, and P. Harrington, 'An Interview with the Black Prophet', *The African Missionary* (Cork), March–April, 1917.

Some of the later bibliography on Harris includes Edmond de Billy, *En Côte d'Ivoire* (Paris, 1931), Thomas Fenton, *Black Harvest* (London, 1956), Margaret Musson, *Prophet Harris: The Amazing Story of Old Pa Union Jack* (Wallingford, Surrey, 1950), Donald Ching, *Ivory Tales* (London, 1950), C. P. Groves, *The Planting of Christianity in Africa* (London, 1958), and B. Holas, *Le Separatisme religieux en Afrique Noire* (Paris, 1965). Other descriptions of Harris's work or its later developments have appeared in Ernest Bruce, 'I grew up with history', *African Challenge* vii, 4, April 1957, D. Desanti, *Côte d'Ivoire* (Lausanne, 1962), R. Grivot, 'Le Cercle de Lahou (Côte d'Ivoire)', *Bulletin de l'Institut Français d'Afrique Noire*, IV, Jan.–Oct. 1942, J. Hartz, 'Le Prophète Harris vu par lui-même', *Devant les sectes non-Chretiennes* (Bruges, 1961), B. Holas, 'Bref aperçu sur les principaux cultes syncrétiques de la Basse Côte d'Ivoire', *Africa*, XXIV, Jan. 1954, A. Roux, 'Un Prophète: Harris', Le Monde Noir, num. sp. 8–9 de *Présence Africaine*, 1955.

For general background there are many valuable references, especially on the religious and sociological background of the African peoples concerned, and with cultural changes among colonial peoples. One might mention in particular Margaret J. Field, *Search for Security* (London, 1960), Margaret Mead, *New Lives for Old* (London, 1956), P. Tempels, *Bantu Philosophy* (Paris, 1959), C. G. Baëta, *Prophetism in Ghana* (London, 1962), A. J. F. Köbben, 'Prophetic movements as an expression of social protest', *International Archives of Ethnography*, XLIX, I, 1960, E. G. Parrinder, *African Traditional Religion* (London, 1962), A. F. C. Wallace, 'Revitalisation movements: some theoretical considerations for their comparative study', *American Anthropologist*, LVIII, 2, April 1956.

As noted above, the official files were apparently not examined by those who wrote on Harris, with the possible exception of two of the earliest, Joseph and Marty. I therefore was excited by discovering a wealth of information in government and missionary society collections. Perhaps I was most fortunate in locating in the National Archives of the Ivory Coast the regular political reports from the *cercles*, as well as informative correspondence. The National Archives of Senegal house a clearly identified file on Harris and later developments of his movement. The National Archives of Ghana contain files and correspondence dealing largely with the effects of Harris's visit. Thanks to the interest of a friend I was able to obtain information on the crucial flag-raising incident, as dealt with by the Liberian courts, from the National Archives of Liberia. In London the Public Record Office was the source of valuable information in General Correspondence and Confidential Prints relating to Liberia, information which threw some light on the tensions in the Republic at the time Harris was sent to prison. Finally I must mention the very great co-operation offered me by the staff at the Methodist Missionary Society in London, in whose files of correspondence and reports was buried a great deal of information on the Harris Movement and its aftermath. I regret that I was not able to gain entry to the several collections of the Société des Missions Africaines; on that account it may be that the Catholic view of the Harris Movement has been slighted.

This bibliography is not an exhaustive one; inevitably many books which supplied ideas or bits of information have not been listed here, but I believe the most valuable material bearing directly upon the Prophet Harris, his life and his movement, are noticed above.

Index